Student Companion to

Edgar Allan POE

Recent Titles in
Student Companions to Classic Writers

Student Companion to

Edgar Allan POE

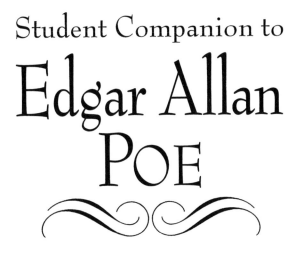

Tony Magistrale

15-84

Student Companions to Classic Writers

Greenwood Press
Westport, Connecticut • London

Library of Congress Cataloging-in-Publication Data

Magistrale, Tony.
    Student companion to Edgar Allan Poe / Tony Magistrale.
        p.   cm.—(Student companions to classic writers, ISSN 1522–7979)
    Includes bibliographical references and index.
    ISBN 0–313–30992–2 (alk. paper)
    1. Poe, Edgar Allan, 1809–1849—Criticism and interpretation.   2. Poe, Edgar Allan,
1809–1849—Examinations—Study guides.   3. Fantasy literature,
American—Examinations—Study guides.   4. Fantasy literature, American—History and
criticism.   I. Title.   II. Series.
PS2638.M24   2001
818'.309—dc21   00–049071

British Library Cataloguing in Publication Data is available.

Library of Congress Catalog Card Number: 00–049071
ISBN: 0–313–30992–2
ISSN: 1522–7979

First published in 2001

Greenwood Press, 88 Post Road West, Westport, CT 06881
An imprint of Greenwood Publishing Group, Inc.
www.greenwood.com

Printed in the United States of America

∞™

The paper used in this book complies with the
Permanent Paper Standard issued by the National
Information Standards Organization (Z39.48–1984).

10 9 8 7 6 5 4 3 2 1

Cover portrait of Edgar Allan Poe reproduced from the Collections of the Library of Congress.

For Professors Frederick S. Frank and Sidney Poger,
my first and last teachers of Poe

Contents

Series Foreword

This series has been designed to meet the needs of students and general readers for accessible literary criticism on the American and world writers most frequently studied and read in the secondary school, community college, and four-year college classrooms. Unlike other works of literary criticism that are written for the specialist and graduate student, or that feature a variety of reprinted scholarly essays on sometimes obscure aspects of the writer's work, the Student Companions to Classic Writers series is carefully crafted to examine each writer's major works fully and in a systematic way, at the level of the non-specialist and general reader. The objective is to enable the reader to gain a deeper understanding of the work and to apply critical thinking skills to the act of reading. The proven format for the volumes in this series was developed by an advisory board of teachers and librarians for a successful series published by Greenwood Press, Critical Companions to Popular Contemporary Writers. Responding to their request for each-to-use and yet challenging literary criticism for students and adult library patrons, Greenwood Press developed a systematic format that is not intimidating but helps the reader to develop the ability to analyze literature.

How does this work? Each volume in the Student Companions to Classic Writers series is written by a subject specialist, an academic who understands students' needs for basic and yet challenging examination of the writer's canon. Each volume begins with a biographical chapter, drawn from published sources, biographies, and autobiographies, that relates the writer's life to his or her work. The next chapter examines the writer's literary heritage, tracing the literary influences of other writers on that writer and explaining and discussing the literary genres into which the writer's work falls. Each of the following chapters examines a major work by the writer, those works most frequently read and studied by high school and college students. Depending on the writer's canon, generally between four and eight major works are examined, each in an individual chapter. The discussion of each work is organized into separate sections on plot development, character development, and major themes. Literary devices and style, narrative point of view, and historical setting are also discussed in turn if pertinent to the work. Each chapter concludes with an alternate critical perspective from which to read the work, such as a psychological or feminist criticism. The critical theory is defined briefly in easy, comprehensible language for the student. Looking at the literature from the point of view of a particular critical approach will help the reader to understand and apply critical theory to the act of reading and analyzing literature.

Of particular value in each volume is the bibliography, which includes a complete bibliography of the writer's works, a selected bibliography of biographical and critical works suitable for students, and lists of reviews of each work examined in the companion, both from the time the literature was originally published and from contemporary sources, all of which will be helpful to readers, teachers, and librarians who would like to consult additional sources.

As a source of literary criticism for the student or for the general reader, this series will help the reader to gain understanding of the writer's work and skill in critical reading.

Preface

The *Student Companion to Edgar Allan Poe* is meant to be used as an introduction to the life, times, and major work of one of America's greatest authors. The contributions of a great author must withstand the test of time, enduring the social, political, or religious context in which his or her canon emerges, as well as the various critical interpretations that are later applied to explain what the literature means. Poe's work has definitely withstood these tests. His best poems and fiction are more popular and carry greater significance now, a century and a half after they were first composed, than they did during his own era. Writing about his own personal demons and highly individualized aesthetics may have made Poe the quintessential Romantic, but his insight into human nature and its infinite capacity for evil suggest that of all the American writers from the nineteenth century, Poe was perhaps closest to understanding the spirit of the century that would follow. In his best work, Poe was all the time conscious of loss, disintegration, darkness, and things ending, just as we are. Poe died totally unaware of how important he would become to subsequent generations of writers, readers, and even artists employing mediums far removed from literature.

The power of truly great literature transcends its creator, and sometimes even the intention the creator had in mind for it. Since Poe's death, his art has attracted interpretations and appreciation from the most unlikely readership. For example, his poetry ("The Raven" and "The Bells" are specific favorites) is memorized by Russian school children, while in Japan, Poe was a major inspiration for imagery and themes used in the Japanese manga (comics) and computer game industry in the 1970s and 1980s. Poe has become, like Shakespeare and Van Gogh, a figure who transcends his time, place, and nationality; he no longer belongs to America, but to the world.

The French Symbolist poets in the nineteenth century were the first to claim Poe as one of their own, in personality as well as aesthetics, and it was primarily Charles Baudelaire's twenty-year commitment to translating Poe into French that made his work available to the non-English-speaking world. The debt to the Baudelaire translations must be viewed as immeasurable, for by the end of the nineteenth century Poe's art had already created a permanent and stunning influence upon world literature. The twentieth century has merely confirmed his status; Poe is a precursor to the Modernist movement, a figure that connects T.S. Eliot back to the French Symbolists and Hart Crane to the role of the poet as a spiritual voyager. Crane's own alcoholism, financial desperation, and self-doubts inspired him in his masterpiece *The Bridge* (1929) to recognize Poe as a mentor, the ultimate figure of the suffering artist whose lasting achievement transcends his personal pain.

Poe was one of those rare literary geniuses who not only labored successfully in multiple genres—poetry, fiction, the essay—but also went on to contribute significantly to defining and exploring the fullest range of possibilities inherent in these genres. Chapter 3 explores the major poems from Poe's canon with special attention to his aesthetic appreciation for verse that inspired a lovely distorted strangeness—employing imagery that is lovely because it is distorted, beautiful because it is so strange. This chapter's concluding "Alternate Reading" section examines the way in which Poe's theories of poetry, as they are articulated in several of his most famous formal essays, serve to inform the specific construction of poems in his canon.

Poe's short fiction offers a broader range of themes and greater psychological complexity than we find in his poetry. Stories such as "A Descent into the Maelström" and "The Island of the Fay," for example, illustrate Poe's ability to transport the reader into fantastic realms of action adventure that take place in wide-open settings. On the other hand, tales such as "The Tell-Tale Heart" and "The Black Cat" are descents into the darkest part of the human psyche, symbolically located in constricted basements and bedrooms, and revealing the human propensity to seek pain rather than tranquility. It is astonishing how many of Poe's stories involve beds and bedrooms not only as settings, but also as a means for committing crimes, effecting escapes, and witnessing supernatural phenomena. Contrasting both these types of narratives are Poe's stories of detection: "The Murders in the Rue Morgue," "The Purloined Letter," and "The Mystery of Marie Roget." These early prototypes of the modern detective genre underscore the struggle between rationality and chaos, always highlighting the superiority of the former over the latter.

Chapter 4 is the first of three to focus on Poe's fictional prose. Each of these chapters subdivides Poe's narratives into distinct categories. Chapter 4 explores the love stories, or what some scholars refer to as Poe's "marriage group": those tales that revolve around interpersonal relationships between men and women, their respective struggles for control over the relationship, and the gender polarities and antagonisms that distinguish these interactions. The chapter further considers these various issues in the context of Poe's adaptation of the vampire theme; unlike the traditional vampire story, however, in Poe the vampire-victim relationship is forever shifting while the usual need for blood is replaced with a gendered quest for psychic domination. This chapter concludes with an Alternate Reading section that introduces a feminist critical approach to the gender dynamics at work in this specific grouping of stories. Poe's women characters are simultaneously oppressed and oppressive; consequently, a feminist reading of their personalities and marital situations offers tremendous interpretative possibilities, especially for counterbalancing the essentialist male viewpoint provided by Poe's first-person narrators.

In chapter 5, Poe's most famous tales of terror and revenge are juxtaposed. These narratives have been placed together because they all revolve around murders and undiluted elements of horror associated with the act of killing. In essence, the stories considered in this chapter represent Poe's greatest contribution to the Gothic tale of terror. Poe's murderers are not so much compulsive killers as they are compulsive talkers. Thus, these tales are also demarcated by a reliance upon first-person male narrators. I am not certain why first-person narratives—in songs as well as fiction—invade the listener/reader's nervous system so effectively, but more than a century and a half after their composition these tales of death and mayhem still possess the power to unnerve even the most jaded of sensibilities. Although they tell their confessional stories in present tense—so the reader feels a direct, nearly vicarious role in the revelation of the crime—these Poe protagonists are actually reflecting back upon past events from the confines of the jail or the asylum, and often within immediate proximity to the gallows. Chapter 5 concludes with a Marxist Alternate Reading of Poe's sociopathic personalities. This interpretation is meant to be both an introduction to Marxism and a reading of Poe's most psychologically disturbing narratives within the social and political contexts of nineteenth-century capitalism. The analysis does not posit that Poe was himself a Marxist, or even that he was sympathetic to Marxist ideology but, rather, that he was more political than most Poe scholars prefer to believe and that the veiled politics found in his fiction were less than patriotic.

The final chapter in this volume counterbalances earlier chapters that center upon Poe's obsessionally distorted criminals. The irrational crimes and self-punishments of the homicidal fantasies found throughout Poe's canon are counterpointed in the rational crime-solving emphases of the detective tale, in which Poe elaborates upon the ratiocinative capabilities of the central character, C. Auguste Dupin. By virtue of his strategic opposition to the criminal, Dupin presents an alternative vision to the violence and madness fomented by Poe's murdering monsters. To highlight this variance, the Alternate Reading section that concludes chapter 6 features a psychoanalytic approach to Poe's detective narratives. Many twentieth-century Poe scholars have applied psychoanalytic interpretations to Poe's characters and fiction. In addition to defining various ways in which psychoanalysis deepens our understanding of Poe's detective tales, this chapter highlights Jacques Lacan's famous essay on "The Purloined Letter" and the further commentary it has inspired.

The student of Poe begins his appreciation of the writer's contribution to the world with the realization that in the course of merely forty years Poe produced an enormous body of work. As chapter 2 of this book attempts to chronicle, over the years Poe has meant different things to different readers. He is at once the progenitor of the modern detective tale, Romantic poet of dissolution and dissipation, conjurer of fantasy and science-fiction dreamscapes, literary psychologist dramatizing case histories of unstable personalities unable to discipline unstable urgings, theoretician of cosmic origins and genre criticism, and an ultimate explorer of the most vast and uncharted landscape known to man: the human mind. Poe was, finally, the American Shakespeare of the lunatic asylum. What he left for those readers stalwart enough to consider without flinching was nothing less than a portrait of ourselves. That this portrait perhaps turns out unsuitable for framing has less to do with the limits of Poe's talents than with the pervasiveness of human depravity and violence.

The author is indebted to many individuals and institutions who contributed to making this book a reality. First, and most important, my editor at Greenwood Press, Lynn Malloy, provided astute editorial commentary and revision advice on each chapter as it was finished. She enriched this volume immeasurably, while her unwavering support of its author helped him to face the computer screen day after day. The manuscript was then further improved by the meticulous copyediting work of Marlowe Bergendoff. Parts of chapter 3 were originally presented as a series of invited lectures at Broward Community College, while chapter 4 began as a paper delivered at the International Conference for the Fantastic in the Arts. The University of Vermont Committee on Research and Scholarship awarded a generous Summer Research Fellowship to complete the writing of this project. For the past decade, students at the University of Vermont—enrolled in untraditional English courses such as "The

Literary Vampire" and "Poe's Children"—provided critical insights that have forever shaped, confirmed, and challenged the author's understanding of Edgar Poe and his canon. Sid Poger, who for several years has team-taught many of these classes with me, also contributed immensely to whatever wisdom is found between these covers (but to none of the mistakes). This is as much their book as it is mine. And lastly, the author offers his sincerest thanks to supportive family and friends—especially Jennifer, Christopher, and Daniel Magistrale and Larry Bennett—who provided frequent and necessary distractions all along the way.

Burlington, Vermont
August 2000

1

Notes Toward a Biography

Was there ever a life sadder than Edgar Allan Poe's? Of course his sadness is part of the famous literary mythology now associated with his work and life: in so many ways Poe was the king of pain, the paragon of the lonely heart of lost love, the archetypical Romantic. His was a life that fluctuated between having been cheated by fate's cruelest machinations and having labored hard to destroy his own best opportunities. He loved, lost, ached, mourned, drank compulsively to ease his sorrow, and struggled with a prodigious genius that was among the greatest of the nineteenth century. He loved the poetry of John Keats, and Poe's life and artistry illustrate the quintessential Keatsian notion of a beautiful bond between love and death. The narrator in Keats's "Ode to a Nightingale" is "half in love with easeful death," and the same can be said about the majority of Poe's fictional characters, as well as Poe himself.

Edgar Allan Poe helped to establish the image of the Romantic artist as a being who not only created art from the essence of his own personal suffering but also came to define himself through this suffering. This quasi-masochistic stance was born, in part, out of social ostracism; the artist was different—insensibility, values, and sense of place in society—from those around him. While other men engaged in "meaningful work" by selling, farming, or laboring with products and profits, the Romantic artist's sole purpose was to create the "Beautiful," and he was not only severely misunderstood by those immersed in the daily dynamics of capitalism, he likewise came to savor both the scorn and rejection of the majority.

But where did this Romantic orientation originate with Poe? As seen in the next chapter, Poe was very much a product of his literary era; the macabre and fantastic strains that dominate his poems and stories were at least partially his inheritance from the Gothic and early Romantic writers he admired from the epoch that preceded his own. But any attempt to explore these qualities in Poe's work would be remiss if it failed to include the importance of Poe's own biography as a means for understanding his literary art, since the dominant themes of suffering, struggle, and loss that readers commonly identify with Poe were at least partially conceived in the experience of daily living.

Edgar Poe was born on January 19, 1809, in Boston in a rooming house at 62 Carver Street. Approximately two years later Edgar lost both his parents. His father, David Poe, was a New York City actor struggling to support a family that consisted of two sons and a wife, Eliza, also an actor. Edgar Poe would come to share several unfortunate characteristics with his biological father: most significantly, a reputation for drunkenness and the inability to ever reach a level of financial prosperity. Burdened by these problems, in addition to a brooding conflict with his parents, a more successful wife on the stage, a series of bad reviews about his own stage work, and two infant children, David Poe disappeared from theatrical life and his young family at the age of twenty-five. None of Poe's biographers have been able to trace where he went, exactly why he left, or whatever became of him.

Only twenty-three years old, Eliza was left to raise her two small boys alone. And for several months after David's departure she worked hard on the New York stage garnering successful reviews. Benefit performances for her were conducted, calling attention to her particular plight and requesting mothers especially to give aid. These gestures of charity were intensely welcomed, for in December 1810, Eliza gave birth to her third child, a daughter, who many biographers have speculated may not have been David's child. By the summer of 1811, Eliza's situation as a working single mother grew so desperate that her health became impaired; she died on December 8. Her children were present at her death. The actual death itself is essential to any study of Poe, since the cause of Eliza Poe's demise was consumption. Her ordeal was both prolonged (lasting several months) and particularly gruesome (choking, profuse bleeding from the mouth, eventual suffocation). These graphic images of death and dying would probably have been enough to animate a lifetime of nightmares for any child. For Poe himself, they would become obsessive components to his art.

After the death of his mother, Edgar was separated from his siblings (he never saw his sister again). Brought into contact with the Poe family during several of the charitable benefits assembled to help Eliza, Frances and John Allan were quick to bring Edgar into their home, although it should be emphasized that Frances had to convince her husband to assume guardianship over

Edgar, and the child was never legally adopted. The three-year-old boy moved into an environment radically different than the one he had shared with his mother and siblings. John Allan was a successful merchant and mercantiler. He was a Scotch immigrant who established the Richmond firm of Ellis and Allan to market Virginia tobacco for European commodities. He was frugal, shrewd, self-disciplined, and rigidly pragmatic about his own life and the lives of others in his family. He did not see, for example, the value of a college education, while Edgar desperately desired it. Some Poe scholars suggest that it was Edgar's enrollment at the University of Virginia, in February 1826, that brought his quarreling with John Allan to a breaking point. Edgar was a student there for only one year, and although he wished to continue, John Allan refused to support him, upbraiding Poe for "eating the bread of Idleness."

At first, Allan treated his foster child kindly if not indulgently, although any real affection came from Allan's wife. Frances was apparently devoted to Poe during his childhood, often taking his side in the frequent arguments between him and her husband. Poe maintained contact with her even after his eventual estrangement from the Allan household and held her in great esteem. Like Poe's biological mother, she was an early example of what women came generally to represent for Edgar: beings who could potentially supply him with the affection and security he so desperately required, but who were never physically strong enough to make love a permanent reality in his life.

During Poe's adolescence, John Allan became increasingly impatient and demanding. John Allan abhorred the decadent "Byronic tendencies" he saw emerging in Poe's personality, while young Poe grew increasingly attracted to the English poet whose impractical Romantic characters and personal rebellious stances stood in direct opposition to Allan's bourgeois values. The Poe-Allan relationship is a saga of mounting mutual dislike that gradually deepened into permanent animosity with distinct overtones of violence. Some accounts actually have Allan threatening Poe with a cudgel during one of their frequent quarrels over money and careers. Poe often sought financial help from his foster father, particularly when his gambling debts grew excessive as an undergraduate at the University of Virginia and the military academy. And certainly a major reason for their deteriorating relationship was Poe's conviction that Allan was never adequate in his response to his foster son's financial needs. It remained Poe's conviction that his foster father's parsimonious attitude forced the son to borrow, gamble, and fall in with a dissolute bunch at both the University of Virginia and West Point. Poe ended up in debt not because he liked to drink and squander, but because, he said, "it was my crime to have no one on Earth who cared for me, or loved me" (Silverman, 1991, 64).

Although there was a superficial reconciliation in February 1829, when Poe returned to Richmond for his foster mother's funeral (like Poe's biological mother, Frances Allan died of consumption), the severe father and prodigal son were permanently estranged after Poe quit the Allan household in March 1827. Upon his death, John Allan excluded Poe from his will by making no mention of him, but did provide for two illegitimate twin sons born in 1830. In an antipatrimonial gesture of defiance, Poe began to sign his name "Edgar A." rather than "Edgar Allan."

John Allan's psychological presence in Poe's troubled life is perhaps as significant as the psychological void caused by David Poe's abandonment. Later, with other men, Poe generally maintained contentious relationships, reenacting the dramatic hostilities engendered from his two father figures. Many of the psychobiographical interpretations of Poe's tales and poems are inspired by the overbearing surrogate father and the missing father figure in his life. The bitter resentments that Poe harbored toward these two central authority figures extended well beyond the death of John Allan in 1834 and David Poe's abandonment, to the point where Edgar may well have recreated these men in his portrayals of the dark fathers and judgmental authority figures that populate his tales, such as the paternal representatives in "Annabel Lee," those "highborn kinsmen [who] came and bore her away from me."

Edgar Allan Poe enlisted in the army in May of 1827. He gave his name as Edgar A. Perry, and registered as twenty-two, although he was only eighteen. In June 1830 he entered West Point. Respected by his peers and tutors, Poe excelled as both a French linguist and mathematician. However, his acrimonious relationship with his foster father continued to haunt him. At the end of 1830, Allan sent what he called his final letter, declaring that he desired no further communication with Edgar. Convinced that John Allan had abandoned him to start a fresh life with a new wife and child, Poe lost interest in his studies and grew weary of the discipline and regimented hours required of cadets. Some Poe biographers have suggested that Edgar only enrolled at West Point out of a desire to curry favorable attention from John Allan; when this failed to work, he lost all interest in the place. After eighteen months of hard work at the academy, Poe decided to quit. He deliberately set out to get expelled, and in January 1831 he was court-martialed and dismissed from West Point for "gross neglect of duties" and "disobedience of orders."

From 1831 to 1835 Poe lived in poverty in Baltimore. He tried unsuccessfully to find work as a schoolteacher, an editorial assistant, and for a spell may have even rejoined the army. During these years, he struggled to make a living, occasionally writing poems but never making enough money to secure a decent diet or purchase sufficiently warm clothing. As his position became more desperate, he drank more excessively, turning to alcohol as a refuge from a world that had treated him with such indifference. Poe's substance abuse problems are part of the public myth associated with his life. There is no question that Poe was an alcoholic, but there is very little evidence that he engaged in using other drugs; liquor was apparently his sole addiction. Throughout his life, his drinking was an omnipresent topic of concern for friends and foes alike. Nathaniel Willis, who befriended Poe in New York City late in Edgar's life, believed that Poe suffered from a certain unfortunate sensibility to alcohol; a single glass of wine could sometimes change his personality drastically, so that he "talked like a man insane." And it surely didn't help that alcohol inflamed Poe's hypersensitive and often vitriolic personality. With the notable exception of George Graham, founder of *Graham's Magazine* and an early defender of Poe, there were very few editorial authority figures in Poe's life with whom he did not openly feud. In addition, many of these altercations were initiated or exacerbated by the inclusion of alcohol. The closer a reader examines Poe's relationships with editors and literary journals throughout his career, the more obvious it becomes that the combination of Poe's incessant drinking and self-defeating urge to solicit aggressive personal conflict contributed greatly to his lifetime of financial stress and worldly misery.

If Poe didn't actively pursue destructive father surrogates out of his coterie of East Coast editors, reviewers, and fellow writers, he turned these males into them, putting himself back into the familiar position of the wayward son dependent upon the whim of their goodwill (Mallin, 120). There emerges from all this a definite pattern to Poe's personal relationships with men in general, but especially to the literary men in his life: an initial period of seldom longer than a year, where Poe's genius would impress and encourage a bonding of sorts. This would always be followed by hostile conflict, usually inflamed by Poe's drinking. An editor or benefactor would demand sobriety; Poe would drink all the more. An abrupt dismissal or break in the relationship would usually follow, engendering deathless animosity on both sides.

It is important for modern readers of Poe, perhaps accustomed to thinking of the publishing world in terms of giant corporate monoliths and best-seller lists, to understand that in the nineteenth century most writers made their living by publishing in periodicals—primarily newspapers and literary journals—rather than in single-volume collections of poems, stories, or a novel. Certainly one explanation for this was the cost of publications: books were more expensive (mass market paperbacks not yet having been invented) and less accessible (there being far fewer libraries with much smaller inventories than what we are accustomed to today). From 1825 to 1850 there occurred a 600 percent increase in new American periodicals, due in no small part to new printing technologies, improvements in eyeglasses, the diffusion of public education, and an easier and wider distribution of printed texts by an expanding railway system (Silverman, 1991, 99). Consequently, most of Edgar Allan Poe's work—his poems, his short tales, his literary essays, and book reviews—were published initially by various periodicals before they were assembled into book volumes. While living in Baltimore in 1831, Poe struggled to launch his own literary career by writing and submitting stories to the Philadelphia *Saturday Courier*. Four years earlier, he had published his first collection of poems, *Tamerlane and Other Poems*, and while he would continue to write verse all through his career, it was clear early on that he could not make a living writing poetry. As a result of his financial condition, Poe turned to composing stories, essays, and book reviews for a wide variety of eastern newspapers and journals.

During his career, Poe wrote an incredible number of book reviews, and on topics so widely diverse (e.g., Lewis Durlacher's *Treatise on Corns, Bunions, the Diseases of Nails, and the General Management of the Feet* and *The Conchologist's First Book; or, A System of Testaceous Melacology*) that it is impossible not to believe that many of these reviews were composed strictly for the money. On the other hand, Poe was also one of the most demanding and thorough readers in America; he set a standard of competence that was a refreshing change from the sentimental nonsense that often passed for literary analysis in his era. His caustic reviews of other writers merited his nickname "Tomahawk." He established himself as a progenitor of American literary criticism, and his insistence that a literary work be read closely as a self-contained aesthetic entity anticipated the criteria of the New Criticism. It is remarkable, considering the daily output of Poe's reviews over the last two decades of his career, that he found the time to do any creative work of his own or to engage the demands of alcoholism. Perhaps the onus of reviewing all the time explains the caustic tone of so many of the reviews. Economic desperation, exploitive editors, and incessant and inflexible deadlines, compounded by the intellectual exhaustion of trying to create his own body of fiction and poetry, were among the demons with which Poe was forced to contend on a daily basis.

Poe's own fiction and poetry likewise appeared in a variety of these contemporary periodicals. And while he was never paid handsomely for this work, newspapers and journals did provide him with an initial forum to display his prodigious talents. Poe was awarded several literary prizes, such as the *Baltimore Saturday Visitor* competition that he won 1833 with "MS. Found in a Bottle." While Poe's creative writing never amounted to much financially, he did manage to generate a certain measure of attention among some of the major literati of his time. For example, although Nathaniel Hawthorne and Poe never met, they did exchange letters and were deeply engaged by each other's fiction. Unlike Hawthorne, Ralph Waldo Emerson was not an admirer of Poe's work, disparagingly referring to the poet Poe as "the jingle man" and dismissing the absence of "moral principles" governing Poe's prose. So while Poe's own literary efforts had both their detractors and admirers, the point is that his work was read during his lifetime, and he became an important literary figure in the eyes of other important writers and critics in the first half of the nineteenth century. The critical attention he did manage to garner, however, represented only a modest inception for Poe's fame; his true worth as a creative artist was to occur posthumously.

From 1835 to 1837, Poe was on the staff of the *Southern Literary Messenger* as book critic and contributing editor. In addition to publishing many early tales and book reviews in the *Messenger*, Poe eventually became the editor of the magazine for about six months in 1836. During Poe's tenure as editor, the *Messenger*'s circulation rose from 500 to 3,500, making it one of America's most popular and influential journals. But during this period, his salary never rose above the original ten dollars per week for which he was originally hired.

Although he became quite knowledgeable about the magazine world of his day, Poe's erratic personality and problems with alcohol kept him from ever rising to other, more permanent positions of editorial management. His relationships with most of these literary periodicals thus remained limited to Poe's contributions as writer and critic. The *Broadway Journal*, for example, republished many revised versions of important Poe stories in the mid-1840s, including "Ligeia," "William Wilson," and "The Tell-Tale Heart." In addition to criticism and reviews, Poe contributed tales and poetry to *Graham's Magazine* from 1840 to 1842; almost every volume of the magazine issued during this period contains a Poe story. A fair assessment of Poe's ambivalent relationship with the periodical world of mid-century America would suggest that Edgar was, on one hand, able to find a way to survive financially as a writer while his work, as I have already discussed, garnered a certain amount of attention. On the other hand, Poe never received more than a subsistence-level income from all these publishing ventures. Moreover, his frustration in watching writers such as Longfellow and Bryant attain critical and financial success, while he continued to struggle with demanding editors, rigid deadlines, and the relegation of his own art to the articles and book reviews he was forced to produce at an almost daily rate, surely inspired Poe's jealousy, particularly over Longfellows's reputation and the fact that he was able to make poetry financially advantageous.

As with his efforts to become a critically acclaimed and financially independent writer, most of Poe's romantic relationships were doomed to failure. An early "engagement" to Elmira Royster [Shelton], for example, ended abruptly when the girls's father rejected Poe as a future son-in-law because his financial prospects were so hazy. But in 1835 Edgar finally got lucky in love and married his first cousin, Virginia Clemm, who was at the time of their union only thirteen years old. Poe's biographers have offered varying interpretations of this marriage. Some have suggested that what Poe wanted most from marriage was to restore some presence of the missing mother figures in his life. Virginia was wife, mother, and sister to Poe—someone to take care of him. But other biographers have argued that this union was more passionate than merely a convenient domestic arrangement would imply—indeed, that Virginia often kissed Poe so passionately in public that Poe found it embarrassing. In any event, his marriage to Virginia, which was to last a little over a decade, brought Poe his closest insights to real happiness by quelling momentarily his quest for someone to fill the void of his omnipresent loneliness.

Poe's marriage, however, did not ease his financial burden; in fact it probably deepened it. Now his writing was not only necessary to his own survival, he worked also to support Virginia and her mother, Maria "Muddy" Clemm, who lived with them in Richmond and New York. Poe labored hard in his multiple roles of creative writer, editorial assistant, and book reviewer, but supplying his own and his family's needs was not easy. Poe devoted much of his free time and salary to educating Virginia, and he was often forced to borrow money from friends and relatives and to entertain wild schemes to raise extra income. Broke and always borrowing, Poe was clearly never very far removed from poverty— even when he was most content personally—and it shadowed him throughout his career. He spoke often of being "ground into the very dust with poverty."

Virginia and Edgar had no children. This fact helped to fuel speculation by biographers such as Marie Bonaparte, who conducted a Freudian inquiry into Poe's lifelong fixation on women as mother surrogates and concluded that Poe was impotent and that his marriage to Virginia was never consummated. Whether or not this speculation is true, Poe's attitude toward his wife always seemed to border on the reverential. As we have traced elsewhere in this biographical sketch, Poe's abrasive personality cost him many opportunities—both personal and financial—but with Virginia he was always apparently kind and solicitous. She was his poetic muse, as Poe wrote a number of poems dedicated to her, and a sweet friend, as much a sister as his wife. Despite their difference in ages, Poe came to rely upon Virginia. This was especially true in the 1840s when periods of depression, illness (caused by an exhaustion that was as much mental as it was physical), alcoholism, and a general despair toward an ungrateful world that largely continued to ignore his genius affected him profoundly.

Virginia and Edgar shared a symbiotic correspondence, perhaps similar to two of Poe's most famous literary couples, Roderick and Madeline Usher. When Virginia began to exhibit signs of physical deterioration occasioned by the onset of tuberculosis, Poe's own corporeal condition also worsened. Poe moved Virginia and her mother to a cottage in Fordham, New York, in 1846 in an effort to find an environment that would be more healthful for Virginia. Unfortunately, the move did nothing to restore her vitality. Having been forced to watch his mother slowly waste from the same disease, Poe was again a helpless observer as a woman he loved deeply was wrenched from him by debilitating illness. Virginia's terrible death agonies grew more intense and violent during the final year of her life. Poe's reaction to her death, which finally occurred on January 30, 1847, underscores several important elements that are noteworthy in light of Poe's fictional concerns. Like one of the bereaved narrators in "Ulalume," "Annabel Lee," "The Raven," or "Lenore," Poe reportedly took to visiting Virginia's burial site late at night, even during inclement weather, stealing from the house in stockinged feet so Virginia's mother would not awaken (Silverman, 1991, 329). In a letter to George Eveleth several months after his wife's passing, Poe described what he experienced in witnessing Virginia's slow demise: "She recovered partially and again I hoped. Each time I felt all the agonies of her death—and at each occasion of the disorder I loved her more dearly and clung to her life with more desperate pertinacity. But I am constitutionally sensitive—nervous in a very unusual degree. I became insane, with long intervals of horrible sanity. During these fits of absolute unconsciousness I drank, God only knows how often or how much" (Ostrom, 356).

First, and most obviously, this response suggests the degree of Poe's alcoholism: whenever he found himself under duress, his first inclination was to turn to the bottle for momentary relief. More significantly, however, this description poses an eerie parallel to the narrator in "Ligeia," as both melancholic husbands watch their respective wives slip in and out of consciousness, balancing precariously between life and death. As seen in more specific detail later in this book, many of Poe's male protagonists have much in common with Poe himself as they are forced to watch beautiful women—wives, sisters, and lovers—suffer mysterious illnesses from which they never recover. The incessant coughing, spitting of blood, and slow detachment from the world that Poe witnessed in losing his mother and wife to tuberculosis, and both at the age of twenty-four, took on an obsessive quality for Poe the writer, since the two most important women in his life essentially "bookended" his artistic career with their strikingly similar deaths. Recurring images of heroines wasting away in the presence of their lovers, participating in an ebb and flow of a life energy that is as painful to watch as it must have been to experience, center Poe's most famous love stories. In most of these tales, as in the letter Poe wrote describing his loss of Virginia, the act of dying forges a greater spiritual bond between the woman and the man attending her suffering. "The agonies of her death" somehow inspire deeper levels of sympathy and correspondence: "and at each occasion of the disorder I loved her more dearly." Poe's fictional heroines, occupying roles similar to Virginia's, conflate and blur the perimeters of wife, sister, lover, and mother in his conceptualization of heterosexual love. The womb is never very far removed from the tomb. Yet, we will soon see that Poe's fictional women seldom rest in peace. They are shockingly reanimated from the tomb, the fantasy of a grieving child who wishes desperately for the magical return of the deceased idealized parent, or as the bereaved lover reconjures his lost soulmate through a poetic imagination fired by grief.

Late in his career, in the essay "The Philosophy of Composition," Poe supplied us with an aesthetic rationale for understanding his fascination with dead and dying women: "The death, then, of a beautiful woman is, unquestionably, the most poetical topic in the world—and equally is it beyond doubt that the lips best suited for such topic are those of a bereaved lover" (1379). This death, for Poe, is unmistakably aligned with a melancholic sensibility, but additionally, a lovely woman's death is "most closely allied to *Beauty*" (1379). As a Romantic, Poe was drawn to occasions where human emotions were stretched to their limitations; in savoring the delicious pain that attends the loss of a lover and the wasteful expulsion of a beautiful woman from the world, the poet found himself in a position to realize his full capacity for emotion. The death of a beautiful woman certainly brings sorrow, but it also brings the grieving poet the most profound level of self-awareness possible. This sensation is to be indulged and savored, for we are never more alive than when we are forced to contemplate our deepest potential for feeling, regardless of the cause. According to Freud, all artistic energies are essentially death-haunted, rooted in pain and grief. These emotions trigger the human imagination and feed it as much as they threaten to warp it. Creative art, then, is an integral part of the process of mourning something or someone in the past. The memory of loss triggers pain, but in turn, that pain gives occasion for the creation of art, and in Poe's case, great art.

In "The Poetic Principle," Poe seems to be implying that when beauty is lost in the death of a woman we love, another kind of terrible beauty is simultaneously born in the contemplation of her loss. For most of us, the concept of grief as a vehicle for making us feel more alive may appear contradictory and maybe even a little perverse. But for Poe, who was "constitutionally sensitive—nervous in a very unusual degree" and who experienced the deaths of beautiful women he loved on three separate occasions, such an orientation was as irrefutable as it was inescapable. Any creative art involves an extension of the artist's nervous system. Presumably, the more nervous the system of the artist, the more intense his or her art.

Poe lived another two years after the death of Virginia, and they were perhaps the most miserable of his life. Various sources attribute Poe's poor condition during 1847–48 to a "brain fever, or congestion," his inability to recover fully—physically, emotionally, and psychologically—from the loss of his wife, a bad diet that continued to erode his health, bursts of uncontrollable anxiety, a diminishing output of work, his increased sense of isolation among the literati of New York, and a desperate need for money. In December 1847, Poe published the poem "Ulalume: A Ballad." That the poem is a thinly veiled autobiographical statement of Poe's despair over the recent loss of Virginia can hardly be doubted. On the first anniversary of Ulalume's death, the narrator visits her tomb at midnight. Remaining true to her memory, the poet finds himself unable to rise up beyond her loss and begin life anew. With his "palsied" thoughts, the poem's protagonist appears drained of the will to live and reminisces nostalgically upon "days when my heart was volcanic" (89). Throughout the poem the narrator is pulled in two conflicting directions: back toward the memory of Ulalume and forward toward the attraction of a new love as represented by Astarte. In the end, the poet apparently resolves this tension by remaining committed to Ulalume's memory. The fact that he does not return from the grave in the ballad's conclusion suggests that he has resigned himself to the death-in-life condition in a realm without his lover.

Poe may well have written in "Ulalume" the ultimate private allegory of his own conflict of mind after Virginia's death over whether he should seek the love of another woman or remain faithful to his wife's memory. For in the summer of 1848, the tension at the heart of "Ulalume" was paralleled in Poe's own life as he began romantic courtships with at least three different women. He proposed to one of these women, Sarah Helen Whitman, in a Providence graveyard. Their romance reached its pinnacle when she agreed to marry Poe but, then decided to terminate the engagement when Poe's drinking alarmed her. In addition, Mrs. Whitman, mother of Sarah, was opposed to the marriage because she believed Poe was after the family fortune. Several literary acquaintances, among them Rufus Griswold, who would later become infamous as Poe's literary executor, wrote scurrilous letters to the Whitman family slandering Poe's personality and warning Sarah against the marriage.

During this tumultuous period, in November 1848, Poe swallowed an ounce of laudanum in Boston in an effort to commit suicide. Laudanum is an opium derivative, weaker than morphine or heroin. In Poe's time, it was a drug dispensed without a doctor's prescription and was used for a variety of maladies, from headache to depression. It was also widely used as a tranquilizer. But the fact that Poe tried to kill himself with this drug may be one of the best indicators we have that Poe was essentially unacquainted with narcotic abuse. For while Poe took enough of this drug for a fatal overdose, he chose to ingest it, and as a consequence it made him very sick but failed to produce the desired death. Before the laudanum had a chance to take effect in Poe's system, he vomited most of the drug on his way to a post office.

In 1848, Poe published *Eureka*, the longest of his nonfictional works. Constructing a cosmological theory based on mathematics, poetics, and intuitive feeling, Poe posited a universe that was moving inward upon itself toward a beautiful last moment of primal nothingness. The opposite of Einstein's ever expanding cosmos governed by immutable physics, Poe's universe is ever contracting and governed by poetic law. Like many of his time, he was concerned with bringing science and religion into some kind of alignment, and as an artist Poe played God, creating—at least theoretically—his own worlds (Bittner, 228). Thematically, *Eureka* is related to Poe's lifelong fascination with transcending the limits of death. At the very least, the work is an acknowledgment that Poe was preparing himself for his own death, which would occur one year later, with the hope that it might be possible to escape the incessant pain of mortal life and find a beautiful alternative in the great beyond.

In July of 1849, Poe returned to Richmond. Always desperate for money, he began a series of lectures, most of them dealing with literary theory (e.g., "The Poetic Principle"), and frequently concluding with a reading of "The Raven," the poem that is almost synonymous with the name of Poe during his own time as well as our own. Poe's recitations of "The Raven" were very well received by the public; one newspaper even commented that his recitation was "very fine, and would do no discredit to any, even the most finished actor" (Silverman, 1991, 424). Poe undertook the lecture circuit with alacrity, for it brought him more money than any of his other literary endeavors, although he apparently came to view the inevitable request to recite "The Raven" as an unwelcome task, perhaps akin to a rock star cajoled by the audience into playing his most famous song at the end of every concert. During these lectures Poe would appear dressed entirely in black, his habitual color even in the heat of a southern summer and regardless of what other daily tasks were to be undertaken.

Shortly after arriving in Richmond, Poe sought out Sarah Elmira Royster Shelton, the same woman he had proposed to twenty years earlier. Poe again wanted very much to marry her, even purchasing a wedding ring in anticipation; Elmira still found Poe a fascinating person, and she considered his proposal seriously and may have even accepted it. Finally, it appeared as if Poe would fill the chasm in his life created by Virginia's death. But Edgar Allan Poe's luck—particularly in love—was never very longlasting. His personal life was star-crossed with women he had loved only to lose: his mother, his foster mother, Virginia Clemm, Sarah Helen Whitman. So now Poe tried one last time with one last woman—Elmira Royster—his first love as a young man, whom he had originally lost in marriage to another man, but who was now available once again. In reality, his intense courtship of her just before his death was probably one final attempt to make peace with the demons of loneliness that had haunted him since Virginia's loss. However, Poe was simply destined to die as he had lived most of his life: alone.

On September 26, 1849, Poe visited Elmira Royster to say good-bye before a planned trip to New York. He complained of not feeling well, and she noted that he left her in a high fever. Poe used this final meeting to press her to get married before his trip; he feared that unless she consented she would never see him again. However, when Poe set out for Baltimore on the first leg of the journey the morning of September 27, he was still a bachelor. No reliable evidence exists to explain what happened to Poe from that morning until October 3, when he was admitted to a Baltimore hospital in a delirious condition. It is known that on September 28, Poe arrived at the home of a Dr. Nathan C. Brooks in Baltimore, intoxicated. The physician was not at home and Poe then disappeared for the next five days. He was found hallucinating and semi-conscious on a Baltimore street near a tavern on October 3 and was then taken to Washington Medical College in a stupor, unaware of who or what had brought him there.

The issue of how Poe died at 5 A.M. on Sunday, October 7, 1849, is a matter that continues to inspire controversy among Poe biographers. The most recent speculation, posited by an American physician named R. Michael Benitez, is that Poe's hospital symptoms—cold perspiration, delirium, trembling, general confusion, and loss of memory—suggest that he was experiencing an advanced case of rabies poisoning. But Poe's death could just as well have been caused by complications associated with various illnesses he may have been suffering from for a long time. It may have been, for example, diabetes or even a brain tumor. Since he was found wandering the streets of Baltimore in inclement weather, and it is known that he left Elmira Royster in Richmond with a high fever, Poe could have died from a pneumonia brought on from exposure to the elements. As a more sinister possibility, Poe might have been drugged sometime during those unaccountable five days in Baltimore, from which he never recovered. The author's belief is that Poe's "demon gin"—his lifelong struggle with alcoholism—is probably the most plausible explanation for the five-day delirium and semiconscious state that eventually produced his demise. Charles Baudelaire, the French Symbolist of whom more will be said in the next chapter, called Poe's death "almost a suicide, a suicide prepared for a long time" (Hyslop, 101). Poe's final hours were apparently his most horrific, a danse macabre in and out of consciousness, like one of his own literary heroines, hallucinating wildly, and shouting repeatedly for the polar explorer Jeremiah Reynolds, whose explorations of the south polar region had inspired Poe's novel, *The Narrative of Arthur Gordon Pym*. Poe died pronouncing his own epitaph: "Lord help my poor soul."

Edgar Allan Poe was buried the next day, October 8, in the Presbyterian Cemetery in Baltimore. As the funeral was hastily arranged, few mourners were present—one of Poe's former classmates at the University of Virginia, a few distant relatives, some curious literary admirers—and there was no display and little ceremony. Edgar Allan Poe was forty years old.

Poe could not have picked a worse literary executor than Rufus Griswold. Poe's antipathies with surrogate-father John Allan can be understood, if ultimately pitied as unfortunate and unnecessary; Allan was at least honest with the boy he never cared enough about to call his son. But Griswold bore his malice and jealousy in secret. Like Iago in Shakespeare's *Othello*, Griswold planned his revenge on Poe with a calculating design. The two men maintained a professional relationship that began in 1841 with Poe's verse being accepted for Griswold's anthology, *Poets and Poetry of America*. Poe invited Griswold's enmity on several occasions when he found fault with this anthology. He most certainly petitioned Griswold for money on at least one occasion and was rebuffed. After Poe's death, however, Griswold enacted his full revenge: he forged several malicious letters he claimed were written by Poe, he published a scathing and libelous obituary for Poe in the *New York Herald Tribune* that began a campaign of posthumous character assassination unequaled in the world of letters, and he wrote to Mrs. Whitman that he "was not [Poe's] friend, nor was he mine" (Bittner, 294). Why Poe named Rufus Griswold his literary executor is anyone's guess—perhaps he believed Griswold to be his friend, perhaps he trusted naively in the man's literary integrity despite past flaws in their relationship. Perhaps Poe simply had no one else to trust.

Among the flagrant lies and libels perpetrated by Griswold in this obituary and in his introduction to the 1850 volume of Poe's collected works were assertions that Poe had been expelled from the University of Virginia, that Poe was a drug addict and drank himself to death, that Poe had tried to seduce John Allan's second wife and maintained sexual relations with his mother-in-law, and that all of Poe's most perverse and depraved fictional characters were really personal confessions. The vicious portrait that Griswold concocted was devoid of sympathy for Poe's unhappy life, much less appreciative of his contribution to American literature. And perhaps worst of all, it became the unofficial biography for the nineteenth and early twentieth centuries. As we look back on Griswold's character assassination, an ironic justice emerges from the fact that Poe has since become one of the giants of American writing—rather than an incarnation of evil—while the man he trusted with his career has rightly earned all the scorn and disrepute he originally tried to assign to Poe. If Montressor, the cryptic narrator in "The Cask of Amontillado," could have witnessed the whole convoluted relationship between Griswold and Poe, he would have been quick to ascertain that final retribution belonged to Poe alone.

2

The Contribution and Legacy of Edgar Allan Poe

There are many Poes. Several years ago, literary critic Daniel Hoffman published *Poe, Poe, Poe, Poe, Poe, Poe, Poe*, a book whose title managed to highlight at least seven of the possible Poes in this hall-of-mirrors-like phenomenon. But there are more Poes than even the Hoffman title calculates. There is Poe the poet, Poe the inventor of detective fiction, Poe the literary critic, Poe the book reviewer and magazine editor/contributor, Poe the author of grotesquely comic sketches, Poe the creator of psychological horror tales. There is Poe the hoaxster, Poe the fantasist, Poe who applied the principles of ciphers, mesmerism, and cryptology. There are just more Poes than can be considered in this single volume.

This chapter takes up the issues of who and what influenced the major themes and priorities found in Poe's poetry and fictional prose. In addition, Poe has become arguably the most influential writer America ever produced. Who are some of his children—those artists who followed Poe chronologically and are indebted to his work? Why do his poems and stories continue to be read and studied in classrooms all over the world? And what is there about the Poe myth that has created an instantly identifiable celebrity for generations, including our own postmodern culture?

DEFINING THE GOTHIC REVOLUTION   1780 – 1800

During the last two decades of the eighteenth century, musicians, painters, and writers all across Europe reacted against the values and aesthetic sensibilities that shaped a century whose core beliefs were rooted in scientific principles, reason, and rationality. The Age of Reason, or the Enlightenment, trusted that in the proper use of the intellect, humans could overcome the urge to commit random acts of evil against themselves and others. According to historian Norman Hampson, the Enlightenment was convinced that the affairs of man were guided by a beneficent God. Man himself was assumed to be good and decent by nature. In addition to the urge toward self-preservation that he shared with animals, man also possessed a natural kindness that one never sees in beasts (99). The eighteenth century was guided by the philosophy of Deism, which argued that God had created a comprehensible universe, set it in motion, and then left it for man to align himself within its perfect harmony. In many ways, the eighteenth century was a harbinger of our own time: its trust in science (the disciplines of physics and chemistry were born in this century), in the powers of reason and enlightened rationality as a means for the governance of all human conduct (novelist Henry Fielding noted that the age described "not men, but manners; not an individual, but a species"), and its commitment to the faith that order and symmetry were superior to chaos and undisciplined emotion (the music of the century culminated in the highly regimented Baroque). Also called the Age of Neoclassicism, the century adhered to Greek and Roman principles that artistic presentations must attend to classical rules. Building edifices, gardens, landscapes (literal as well as those painted or described) had to conform to precepts of uniformity, proportion, and order; art should be designed to reflect the symmetry of a stable and comprehensible universe.

The Gothic was born out of, and as a reaction to, the Age of Reason. The bright lights that illuminated the Neoclassical laboratory went out when the Gothic was ushered in. If the science of the Enlightenment emphasized the conscious, rational side of man, the Gothic suggested that the unconscious, irrational side is just as powerful—if not more so because there exist no perimeters in the realm of the unfettered imagination. The generation of Gothic authors, painters, and musicians—roughly dominating the last two decades of the eighteenth century—with their tormented skepticism regarding the universality of rationality and natural law, lay the foundations for the antivisions of Keats, Byron, and the other dark Romantics, including Poe, who would emerge in the early nineteenth century. In place of reason's belief in order and self-discipline, the Gothic understood that both human nature and the natural world itself could not be so easily regulated, that we are essentially ambivalent and contradictory beings inhabiting a volatile world. Both man and nature itself, if given the alternative, appeared less likely to perform benevolent deeds than acts of perversity and destruction. So in most Gothic texts, anxiety stimulates pleasure, violence creates delight, horror shapes reality. The Gothic became synonymous with guilt, terror, unconscious and obsessive urges, and individual transgressions against moral and social codes.

The typical Gothic novel of the 1790s featured an aristocratic, self-absorbed male, usually the owner or caretaker of a castle or mansion, handsome but mysterious, charming but socially estranged, whose isolated world is to some degree compromised by the intrusion of a young woman. The chaste Gothic maiden, the sexual foil to the Gothic male villain, created a sympathetic bond with the bourgeois female reading audience of the time: she is simultaneously attracted to and repulsed by the male she encounters in her various fictional roles as governess, distant relative, neighbor, or innocent visitor to the secluded Gothic castle. The rest of the novel, depending upon the author producing it, either revolves around the Gothic maid's hyperactive imagination (e.g., the novels of Mrs. Ann Radcliffe) as her romantic fantasies are systematically stimulated and then dispelled, or else the story centers on the very real and dangerous male pursuit of female distress (e.g., the novels of the Marquis de Sade and Matthew Lewis). In those Gothic narratives where evil reigns, the text is often male villain-centered, while in those tales where good wins out in the end, the novel is conversely maiden-centered. In either case, here we have the fundamental plotline of Gothic crisis: a trembling maiden depicted in some stage of quasi-hysterical flight into or from a dream landscape in which anything can happen and probably will. The Gothic novel highlighted a surreal and superanimated universe out of control, the sexes unable to communicate with one another, an overindulgence of emotion, the relentless pursuit of psychosexual obsessions, and the language of anguish and defiance.

While most of the eighteenth century advocated a pure and uniform view of nature, the Gothic, of course, was attracted to its opposite: nature in its wildest forms. Awe and mystery of the natural world replaced the Enlightenment's belief that nature was best presented as a flat and symmetrical mirror to human homogeneity. The Gothic, on the other hand, takes us into deep forests, across limitless mountain ranges, vast tracks of snow, and, when forced indoors, down dark, seldom-traveled winding corridors and subterranean passageways. Indeed, the interior dwellings of the Gothic are meant to suggest the twisted, convoluted, and highly individualized psychology of the mind itself: nothing is ever clearly understood, and the reader, like the wanderer across a Gothic landscape, is always in danger of getting lost. In the first Gothic text, Horace Walpole's, *The Castle of Otranto*, the novel moves ever more out of narrative control as its personalities enter into greater levels of hysterical confusion. The text's physical geography grows correspondingly darker and more confined. This continues to the point where the major action of the novel actually moves underground, into the twisted and convoluted hallways that honeycomb the subterranean environment of Castle Otranto. Literary critic Frederick S. Frank has posited that "Gothic architecture is imbued with the character and will of its former owners. Place becomes personality, as every corner and dark recess of the Gothic castle exudes a remorseless aliveness, a vile intelligence, and unnatural biology of walls" (14).

In order to understand properly the fiction of Edgar Allan Poe—especially his poetry and tales of horror, detection, and suspense-fantasy—it is first necessary to understand the precepts of eighteenth-century Gothicism and the generation of Romantic proponents who preceded Poe. When Poe produced his major body of work during the 1830s and 1840s, the Gothic revolution in literature and art had all but exhausted itself; its major energies were subsumed into the Romantic movement. But as was the case with the English Romantic poets themselves whom Poe most admired from his youth—Keats and Byron in particular—the Gothic came to exert a tremendous influence in Poe's use of setting, gendered relationships, claustrophobic environments that mirror the internal workings of the human mind under duress. The eccentric and nightmarish interior worlds that characterize Poe's most famous horror stories, for example, neatly parallel Gothic sensibilities that reveled in a particular appreciation for spectacles of violence, human perversity, supernatural occurrences, and a special species of grotesquerie.

Poe certainly inherited many of his Gothic propensities by way of his close reading of Romantic poets such as Keats and Byron, but Poe also shared an even more direct link to the Gothic in his awareness of the genre's primary source-work. He had read carefully the work of Horace Walpole, for example, and several critics have proposed that the supernaturalism of the first Gothic novel was a definite inspirational model for the collapse of Poe's mansion in "The Fall of the House of Usher." In addition, Poe found inspiration for many of his exotic settings and themes from his appreciation of William Beckford's Gothic fantasy *Vathek: An Arabian Tale*. Beckford's narrative is mentioned in several of Poe's works including "The Premature Burial," "Landor's Cottage," and *Marginalia*.

In addition to his profound debt to the British Gothics, Poe imitated the fantastic supernaturalism of German Romantic literature and art. Both Ligeia and Morella, two of Poe's more erudite female characters, are said to be well versed in mystical German literature and philosophy. Indeed, Poe frequently employed the terms *Germanic, metaphysical* (or spiritualism), and *mystical* nearly synonymously. Although Poe neither read nor spoke German, and thus was acquainted with German literature only in translation, his consistent reliance upon Germanic elements and atmospheric effects promoted Poe biographer and French poet Charles Baudelaire to call Poe's sensibilities "sometimes so profoundly Germanic" (Hansen-Pollin, 9, 104–5). In his preface to *Tales of the Grotesque and Arabesque* (1839), Poe felt compelled to defend himself against charges raised by reviewers that his tales were derivative of German Gothic models. Poe responded with the famous line that his brand of "terror is not of Germany, but of the soul," a disclaimer that is equal parts fiction and truth, and ultimately more an effort by Poe to defend himself against charges of possible plagiarism than literary indebtedness.

Poe's early story "Metzengerstein: A Tale in Imitation of the German," features many of the sensationalist devices that characterized the German literary "shocker" prevalent in international magazines of the 1830s and 1840s. Popular literary taste of the American reading public helped to create a mass market for the short fantastic story refined and popularized by German romantics such as Ludwig Tieck and E.T.A. Hoffmann. In his roles as magazine editor and book reviewer, Poe would have been acutely aware of the popularity of these stories. Hoffmann's tales of grotesque fantasy are often mentioned by Poe scholars as forerunners of Poe's work.

More important than documenting the wealth of specific evidence that establishes European Gothicism's influence on Poe, however, is the need to show how he adapted the Gothic to his own ends, shaping the genre as much as the genre had shaped him. Chapter 4 of this book discusses specific examples of Poe's horror tales. But for now, let us consider some general characteristics of Poe's horror art. In addition to recycling an earlier generation's well-established paraphernalia of haunted mansions, enclosed spaces, mysterious ghosts and vampiric phenomena, chaste maidens and psychosexually obsessed males, exactly how did Poe reconfigure the Gothic for his own purposes? In other words, how did Poe actually advance the form by pushing horror to a higher plane?

When the Gothic crossed the Atlantic to American shores in the hands of Poe, it took on a psychological, cerebral slant. Typically, very little action takes place in a Poe story; the real energies are mental: the self tearing at the self. Poe's poetry is typified by a pervasive sense of sadness—a lost love or the abrupt transition back to reality from a visionary landscape. His tales, on the other hand, center not on sadness nor the decadent splendors of a haunted and haunting landscape but on encroaching madness: the complex spectrum of aberrant psychological motivation ranging from sadomasochistic impulses ("The Tell-Tale Heart" and "The Cask of Amontillado") and object fixations ("Berenice," "Ligeia," and "The Black Cat") to guilt sublimation in the form of premature burials ("Usher" and "The Premature Burial") and the perversity of self-loathing ("William Wilson" and "The Imp of the Perverse"). By depicting unstable psyches unable to discipline their darkest urges, his best tales thrust even the most reluctant reader into the demented interior realms of his characters. As literary and social critic Mark Edmundson has noted, "Poe took the already violent modes of revolutionary British Gothic and invested them with an intensity that is altogether American" (71). If the Gothic novel threatened the status quo by unleashing a virtual asylum of sociopathic males, Poe was the first to tell the tale of horror from the sociopath's perspective, to shift the point of view from victim to victimizer. Poe speaks the language of the lunatic asylum. He writes of a compressed world populated by psyches out of control. His unprecedented success at evoking conditions of intense psychological distress yielded a body of fiction that still manages to disconcert modern audiences thoroughly acclimated to audiovisual violence and gore.

One of the most significant elements that Poe inherited from his Gothic forefathers, and went on to sharpen to the point of near suffocating exactitude, was an emphasis on the biology of place. Poe's tales and many of his poems are set in architecture that is invigorated with an infernal energy of its own. In Poe, however, the machinery of the Gothic house or castle always parallels the haunted psyche of the main character. Place, in other words, becomes immediately identifiable with personality. Like their Gothic ancestors from the eighteenth century, the male narrators in many of Poe's stories can't and don't subsist outside the sequestered and heavily perfumed spheres in which they dwell. In the tale "The Fall of the House of Usher," Roderick Usher's psychological deterioration, as well as the dissolution of the Usher lineage, is mirrored in the decaying physical structure of the house itself. When Roderick's sister Madeline falls atop him at the story's climax, the House of Usher appears to respond directly to their unholy union as its walls crumble and collapse. In "The Masque of the Red Death," Prince Prospero establishes an exclusive and secluded world of pleasure and perpetual revelry. The rooms within his self-enclosed castle mirror Prospero's core selfishness, as he has sought sanctuary for his friends and himself against a raging plague that has devastated the rest of his kingdom: "Security [was] within. Without was the 'Red Death.' . . . The external world could take care of itself" (485).

INSPECTING POE: THE DETECTIVE TRADITION

It is certain that Poe's major reputation and greatest influence as a writer come as a result of his contributions as a Gothic artist. But as argued elsewhere in this book, there are many Poes, and one of the most important is Poe the creator of the detective story, a genre that employs rational processes as a counterpoint to the terror and madness that characterize the typical Gothic tale. Poe remained fascinated with the concept of the divided self. Tales such as "The Imp of the Perverse," "The Tell-Tale Heart," and "William Wilson," among many others, suggest that human nature is divided and that this split may underscore a certain necessary balance of opposing forces. This division or split is not just present in Poe's fictional narrators and plots; this same contradictory propensity is evident in the very genres where Poe chose to work. From the eighteenth century, Poe inherited both the Gothic repudiation of a rational and ordered universe by forces beyond our ability to control (the creation of the horror story) and the Neoclassical impulse toward reason and rationality as embodied in the creation of the detective tale. Unlike the Gothic's tendency toward chaos and upheaval, the detective story confronts worldly chaos with a rational mind still left working from the Age of Reason. If the Gothic monster is in rebellion from the order that characterized the eighteenth century, the detective suggests that the rational mind is powerful enough to overcome even the darkest urges of human nature.

Chapter 6 discusses Poe's detective fiction, and in particular C. Auguste Dupin, the world's first literary sleuth. His most significant contribution to the art of crime solving is his mental acuity—a higher form of reasoning that permits him insights into criminal activity that others have overlooked or dismissed as irrelevant. Dupin solves crimes in part from his ability to identify with the criminal mind. He is capable of empathizing with the criminal psyche because Dupin himself remains essentially isolated from the social world. For him, solving a crime is like deciphering a difficult poem or cryptic code; perhaps Dupin's origins are best traced back to Poe's boyhood fascination with cryptograms and puzzles. The detective is essentially disinterested in what happens to the criminal after he is caught, that is, whether he is rehabilitated or even put in prison. Dupin's interests are purely self-motivated and self-defined: can he outwit a criminal's psyche and crack the case?

The literary detectives that follow Dupin make up a long list. The nineteenth-century British novelist, Arthur Conan Doyle, modeled many of Sherlock Holmes's detective traits on Poe's Dupin, including the tacit denigration of fumbling police methods of investigation and solution, the reliance upon super reason, the eccentric and solitary personalities of the detectives themselves, and their peculiar attachment to loyal associates who serve to document the successes of their brilliant mentors. As the detective genre has grown in popularity in the twentieth century, Dupin's unique psychic attributes can be found surfacing in detectives such as Will Graham in Thomas Harris's novel *Red Dragon*. Graham possesses the unenviable gift of being able to identity with the murderous design of Francis Dolarhyde, the novel's serial killer that he must capture. To do so, Graham descends into the darkest regions of his own psyche, forging an intense Dupin-like identification with the criminal in order to apprehend him. In *Mystery*, Peter Straub's detective Lamont von Heilitz inherits the intellectual tradition of detective work that Dupin and Holmes established a century earlier. Von Heilitz approaches crimes as puzzles to be solved, and in Straub's later novel, *The Throat*, von Heilitz's role is assumed by yet another intellectual detective, Tom Pasmore.

Dupin's rational and analytical approach to crime solving also inspired the development of the "police procedural" type of detective story, whose most noted practitioners include Sara Paretsky and Ed McBain and whose methods are followed punctiliously by such television programs as *Homicide, NYPD Blue, Law and Order*, and *Hill Street Blues*.

THE COMIC AND SEAFARING POE

The *Student Companion to Edgar Allan Poe* is meant to aid students who are either being introduced to Poe's canon for the first time, or desire to pursue further their own interpretive research into his work. Thus, this volume's deliberate choice of poems and stories represent those most frequently published in anthologies of American literature or in abbreviated collections of selected Poe works. Because of this emphasis, the student reader of this volume will, unfortunately, find no mention either of Poe's large collection of comic sketches or his only novel, *The Narrative of Arthur Gordon Pym* (1838).

Those who wish to acquaint themselves with a more complete understanding of Edgar Allan Poe should definitely undertake a reading of his lesser-known comic stories such as "The Devil in the Belfry," "King Pest," "A Predicament," and "Never Bet the Devil Your Head." Everything that Poe carried out in a serious vein in the homicidal and suicidal fantasies and detective tales he also performed in quite another key in his comedies, which constitute a large portion of his short story output. These tales are seldom included in English classes or in literature anthologies because course time constraints usually limit an instructor to assigning only those poems and stories that over the years have contributed to Poe's famous reputation as the King of the Macabre. But Poe's comic pieces are as essential to a comprehension of his art as the serious horror tales. In fact Poe's inimitable brand of comedy often blurs the line separating horror and hilarity, the grotesque and the sublime, to the point where characters find themselves wandering aimlessly in a universe that makes absolutely no sense. Despite the commonplace maxim that comedy and tragedy are related, in Poe elements of horror are more often bound up with comedy than are elements of tragedy. The two in fact cross-fertilize and inter-define one another. Comedy is revealed in the reader's recognition of life's frequently cruel absurdities, while the horror unfolds when Poe's protagonists come to realize that they are fatally entrapped.

In many ways, Poe's comic formulations anticipate the theory of the *carnivalesque* as it would be formulated nearly a century later by the Russian literary theorist, Mikhail Bakhtin (1895–1975). Bakhtin's analysis of the medieval carnival draws comedy and horror together since, in their most excessive forms, they both emphasize grotesque exaggerations of the body, particularly its degradation. Poe's comic sketches dramatize what Bahktin was first to notice about the tradition of the pre-Lent carnival: namely, that mocking and misrule reign in their subversion of routine and established reality.

Poe's only novel, *The Narrative of Arthur Gordon Pym*, is also worthy of some elaboration. *Pym* is unique among Poe's more traditional landlocked narratives in that the novel is set exclusively upon the ocean. Although Pym is subjected to a series of horrifying events—largely because of his thirst for excitement—his youthful innocence insulates him from being psychologically destroyed by the realities of his fatal voyage. Told as a series of entries from Pym's journal, the novel is highly episodic with the dangerous sea journey itself as the sole unifying feature. The work is actually less a novel than a series of action scenes showing characters in crisis interrelated only by the device of the sea journey itself. The various boats that are used to transport Pym across oceans and rivers have much in common with the author's descriptions of sinister places in tales such as "Usher" and "The Pit and the Pendulum." Shadowy and surreal, these floating haunted houses are enveloped in an eerie haze, and they transport Pym into the darkest recesses of his imagination.

The novel, then, hovers on the edge of nightmare, a flow of horrific occurrences that tends alternately to wash over and overwhelm both Pym and the reader. After experiencing a series of terrifying episodes that include cannibalism, a violent sea storm, mutiny, and the savagery of island natives, the journal concludes in a final confrontation between Pym and an enormous figure, white as snow, that rises up from the sea in front of his boat. Many critics have presented various interpretations of the novel's final scene, some linking it to the white whale in Melville's own sea-tale, *Moby Dick*, but none has yet produced a totally satisfying explanation of the book's final mysterious figure of white.

POE'S LITERARY LEGACY

While this chapter will provide the reader with at least a broad representative sampling of the various media arts that have been affected by Poe's influence, clearly his greatest legacy remains in the literary realm. Nearly every important writer that followed Poe, representing virtually every national literature, was at least acquainted with him, and those who were not directly shaped by his vision were forced in some way to acknowledge it, if only in an act of repudiation. At the 1999 International Edgar Allan Poe Conference held in Richmond, Virginia, Poe's literary impact abroad was the central focus of many papers that were delivered by American and international scholars. Some of the paper topics included: "Poe and Latin American Literature," " 'The Man That Was Used Up' as a Subtext for Shuji Terayama's Japanese Musical *The Miraculous Mandarin*," and "North of Poe: Edgar Allan Poe and the Canadian Literary Imagination." (Those readers interested in a more detailed and extensive treatment than is afforded in this chapter regarding Poe's influence on world literature should consult Lois Davis Vines's excellent book, *Poe Abroad: Influence, Reputation, Affinities.*)

As mentioned in the preceding chapter, Poe's reputation and importance as a writer were initially rescued from the vicious lies of his literary executor, Rufus Griswold, by the dedicated efforts of the French poet Charles Baudelaire, who purportedly greeted each morning with a prayer to "the great god Edgar Poe." Poe's impact upon nineteenth-century French literature was nothing less than profound and immediate. Not only was Poe the first American artist that Europe took seriously, he was also one of the few American spirits (actor Jerry Lewis perhaps the other notable exception) that French culture has embraced without qualifications. Baudelaire wrote the first European biography of Poe, *Edgar Poe, His Life and His Works* (1856), and invested twenty years translating five volumes of Poe tales, literary essays and prefaces, and *Eureka* into French. His own collection of poetry, *Flowers of Evil* (1861), was written as Baudelaire was translating Poe's tales and their prefaces; consequently, many of these poems show lines shaped by his reading of Poe. Inspired by Baudelaire's efforts in rendering the tales into French, his younger contemporary, Stéphane Mallarmé, spent thirty years translating Poe's poetry into French; while Paul Valéry, to whom Baudelaire and Mallarmé left little to translate, worked upon Poe's essays. Each might have said, as Mallarmé did in 1885, that he had learned English for the sole reason "to read Poe better" (Lawler, 96). Until well into the twentieth century, these French translations and accompanying literary criticism were the source of Poe's literary reputation in France, throughout the rest of Europe, and around the world. Poe's canon was translated into French by three of France's greatest writers and was then rendered into many other languages from these adaptations. Had authors of lesser talent, dedication, and reputation attempted such an ambitious undertaking, Poe's literary fate might have been quite different (Vines 169).

From the very beginning, the French, particularly Baudelaire, were stunned by Poe. Baudelaire did not read Poe as many modern critics have, as a psychologically unstable, or even shallow genius. Instead, he saw in Poe the consummate figure of the artist struggling against bourgeois culture as though trapped in "a vast prison in which he [Poe] ran about with the fevered restlessness of a creature born to breathe the air of a sweeter-scented world" (70). In Poe tales such as "The Imp of the Perverse" and "A Man of the Crowd," Baudelaire found absolute confirmation for his core belief—most gracefully articulated in the poems of *Flowers of Evil*—that the modern city had become a place devoid of meaningful communication and even social life. Baudelaire became convinced that in these tales Poe had invented the first flâneur, a nineteenth-century gentleman who "feels everywhere at home; [who] sees the world, is at the center of the world, and yet remains hidden from the world" (9).

In the latter decades of the nineteenth century, Poe's importance crossed the channel from France to help shape the aesthetics of the English Pre-Raphaelites: Charles Swinburne, Dante Gabriel Rossetti, Aubrey Beardsley, and Oscar Wilde. The highly literate Beardsley was inspired by Poe's themes of fantastic excess and the beauty of strangeness. Many of Beardsley's drawings express visually the abstract sentiments of Poe's heavily burdened narrators and the imperious gaze of his mysterious femme fatales. Oscar Wilde's novel, *The Picture of Dorian Gray*, borrows from two of Poe's short stories. In its supernatural fusing of painting and life, Wilde is indebted to Poe's "The Oval Portrait," while his creation of a dual or double personality in the novel suggests the importance of "William Wilson." The poet Swinburne often berated Americans for failing "to show public reverence" for Poe. Swinburne much admired Poe's poem "The City in the Sea" and found the lines "Whose wreathed friezes intertwine/ The viol, the violet, and the vine" a perfect embodiment of his belief that poetry should be a synthesis of sensual sound and sensuous imagery. Robert Louis Stevenson's *The Strange Case of Dr. Jekyll and Mr. Hyde* is everywhere indebted to Poe's "William Wilson" and its theme of the split self. The fact that *Jekyll and Hyde* is often interpreted as a tale of substance abuse also suggests a familiarity with Poe's own life and employment of drugs and alcohol in tales such as "The Black Cat" and "Ligeia" as a means for producing radical character transformations.

Nineteenth-century Russia was highly attentive to French cultural trends, so it should come as no surprise that Edgar Allan Poe reached Russia initially through Baudelaire's French translations. Feodor Dostoevski's translations of "The Black Cat," "The Tell-Tale Heart," and "The Devil in the Belfry" in 1861 marked the beginning of a fecund literary influence. Dostoevski, arguably the important novelist of nineteenth-century Russia, found many qualities in Poe's art that corresponded to his own literary efforts. A deep intellectual kinship shared by the two writers can be gleaned from Dostoevski's observation that "Poe describes the inner state of [a] person with marvelous acumen and amazing realism" (Boyle, 21). Concerned with dramatizing the spiritual essence of man in conflict with himself and his gods, Dostoevski was intrigued with the psychological implications in Poe's work. The novelist read Poe as a writer who "almost always takes the most exceptional actuality, places his hero in the most exceptional external or psychological position, and with what power of penetration, with what striking verity does he tell the state of that man's soul" (Grossman, 33).

It is certain that Dostoevski borrowed much from Poe's criminals and their artful and artless acts of murdering. The protagonists in both *Notes from the Underground* (1864) and *Crime and Punishment* (1866) follow closely the argument of Poe's narrator in "The Imp of the Perverse," that man will always behave in a self-destructive manner. For Poe, this was a sign of his inherent fallen nature, but Dostoevski went beyond this to see acts against oneself as something more positive—a manifestation of freedom, a sign that human beings are neither predictable nor guided exclusively by self-interest. But it was not just the criminal psyche as portrayed by Poe that intrigued the great Russian novelist. Dostoevski's shrewd and almost compassionate detective Porfiry Petrovitch, the inspector of police in *Crime and Punishment,* is endowed with the intellectual acuity of Poe's C. Auguste Dupin to which Dostoevski adds a highly developed moral consciousness.

In addition to Dostoevski's appreciation of Poe, Ivan Turgenev, another significant figure in the Russian literati of Dostoevski's generation, was acquainted with Poe and especially interested in the latter's bizarre love stories dealing with the phenomenon of "love after death." Turgenev's story "Faust" suggests that the Russian writer may have drawn on "Ligeia" and "Morella" for certain features (Grossman, 57–59).

Parallels with Poe's Gothic life and Gothic art are numerous and inescapable in the life and supernatural fiction of Izumi Kyoka, the finest Japanese Gothic writer of the Meiji period (1868–1912). Like Poe, Kyoka is a central figure in a vigorous Gothic tradition that has flourished in Japanese literature beginning with the work of Ueda Akinari in the eighteenth century. Sharing many features of western Gothicism, both Kyoka and Akinari concentrated their Gothic vision on assertions of the special and spiritual side of life in opposition to the materialism, realism, and martial severity of their Japanese societies. In Kyoka's case, his Gothic can often be understood as a reaction to the oppressive position allotted to women in Japanese life. In "The Surgery Room," one of his earliest Gothic pieces and perhaps his best, the narrator is an observer in the operating chamber where the beautiful Countess Kifune awaits the descent of the surgeon's scalpel having refused to receive any anesthetic for fear of revealing a deeply held secret while unconscious under the drug. To the narrator, she seems already to be a lovely, virginal corpse. Poe's mother in her funeral shroud or consumptive wife Virginia in the diseased beauty of her final hours come immediately to mind. In addition, the reader of Poe's fiction also recalls Madeline Usher, Ligeia, and Berenice, those half-dead female revenants who cling to some semblance of life even though their faces are drained of color. Poe's influence was likewise decisive in the development of short fiction in Japan, particularly in the work of Akutagawa Ryunosuke, who presented tales of terror and the grotesque set in turn-of-the-twentieth-century Japan. After the Second World War, perhaps reflecting Poe's fascination with alienated women who are both angry and oppressed, Poe became a primary interest for *Seito,* the first and most radical feminist journal published in Japan, as twelve translations of his tales appeared consecutively in almost every issue throughout the journal's duration (Lippit, 138).

POE'S AMERICAN FACE

Nineteenth-century American visual artists and writers were perhaps less in-clined to recognize Poe's genius and thus reveal less of an influence than the rest of the world. While he was known by his American contemporaries and many of the authors who immediately followed him, it is clear that Poe's reputation as a great writer was initially forged in Europe. It was not until the twentieth century that the United States began to bestow upon Poe the artistic status he had gar-nered in Europe and Russia since his death. More than fifty years ago, the literary critic Allen Tate posited that "The American case against Poe, until the first World War, rested upon his moral indifference, or his limited moral range" (42). His nineteenth-century countrymen, concerned with documenting explora-tions into the North American wilderness, may also have found Poe's weird tales too claustrophobic, too introverted, too weird. Some were dissuaded from tak-ing Poe seriously because of Rufus Griswold's success in associating Poe with drug addiction and insanity. But maybe it finally came down to a fundamental philosophical difference, as Poe's decadent pessimism contrasts sharply with the spirit of American optimism, most notably articulated by transcendental philos-opher Ralph Waldo Emerson, and appears much more at home within the Euro-pean villages and decayed aristocratic mansions inhabited by so many of his characters. As literary critic Harold Bloom has observed, "[S]elf-reliance, the Emersonian answer to Original Sin, does not exist in the Poe cosmos, where you necessarily start out damned, doomed, and dismal" (284).

In any event, Poe did not become recognized as a writer of major impor-tance in his own country until the twentieth century when his use of symbols and images to suggest rather than state the complex range of psychological conditions and emotions was first appreciated by the Modernist and specifi-cally the Imagist movements. The Modernists were attracted to Poe because of his unromantic and amoral perspective on human nature, his personal and lit-erary alienation from society, and his views on the essential isolation of the in-dividual. They came to recognize that Poe's grotesque portraits do not simply *reflect* real experience; they *are* real experience, because they externalize an in-ner vision of reality. In their general strategic retreat from what they viewed as the puritanism of Victorian sexuality and tradition, early Modernists of the twentieth century found in Poe a writer who shared many of their own rebel-lions, particularly, as articulated by T.S. Eliot, that "damnation itself is an im-mediate form of salvation—salvation from the ennui of modern life, because it at least gives some significance to living" (Hoffman, 53).

As has been the case in tracing Poe's importance internationally, in the United States his influence extends to mainstream authors as well as to special-ists within the Gothic genre. For example, writers as diverse as Richard Wright,

Flannery O'Connor, and Gore Vidal borrow significantly from Poe's canon. Wright discovered Poe early in his career; his politically charged 1940 novel *Native Son* often crosses over into the realm of the horror tale where Poe's influence is apparent in scenic construction, language, and the symbolic use of cats. Gore Vidal was likewise introduced to Poe as a child whose reading habits and enthusiasm were inspired by his grandfather: "Luckily, he got me into Poe, who, as Allen Ginsberg and I were to agree, is the primal fount of American literature, as the French discovered long before we did" (258). Flannery O'Connor, on the other hand, was drawn to Poe's comic sketches, where her fusion of the grotesque and horrible with the comic and ludicrous is frequently compared to Poe. It is hardly possible to read any of her Georgia Gothic tales and novels without finding the southern-bred Poe's influence and inspiration a deeply engrained feature of both her style and themes.

In 1945, H.P. Lovecraft, himself a master of the fantastic tale, published *Supernatural Horror in Literature*, a book of literary criticism on the genre that devoted its only single-author chapter to Poe. Lovecraft appreciated Poe as a writer of psychological terror, insisting, "Whatever his limitations, Poe does that which no one else ever did or could have done; and to him we owe the modern horror-story in its final and perfected state" (52–53). Lovecraft's own fictional narratives owe much to Poe, particularly in their mutual efforts to liberate horror art from stereotyped conventions, concentrating instead upon the creation of new mythologies that tend to emphasize human insignificance in a horrific and essentially incomprehensible universe. Tales such as "The Outsider," "The Dunwich Horror," and "The Rats in the Walls" show Poe's influence on Lovecraft in terms of style and language usage as well as in the very mechanics and physiology of fear and strangeness.

The jump from Lovecraft to contemporary writers working in the genre of the American horror tale is less a leap than a short stumble. We find Poe's legacy still going strong all through the canons of Thomas Harris, Ray Bradbury, Clive Barker, Stephen King, Peter Straub, and Joyce Carol Oates. A section of Bradbury's 1950 collection *The Martian Chronicles*, is entitled "April 2005: Usher II" and features a resurrected Usher mansion constructed in defiance of some future society in which "all the tales of terror and fantasy and horror were burned" (105). Best-selling British novelist, Clive Barker, like so many of Poe's progeny, was introduced to the fiction when he was a child, and his literary life was inimitably transformed: "One of the first books of *fantastique* fiction I purchased was Poe's *Tales of Mystery and Imagination*, in a paperback edition with a lurid cover. It cost, if memory serves, 2/6d. I was ten or so and this seemed a fortune. But then treasure houses are seldom cheap. And I thought, 'My god! There are adults out there who have the same kind of dreams that I have'" (Barker and Jones, 214). And in the "Afterword" to her short story collection

Haunted: Tales of the Grotesque, Joyce Carol Oates likewise explicitly dates a debt to Poe going back to childhood. Her sentiments could easily be applied to most contemporary writers of horror fiction: "Who has not been influenced by Poe?—however obliquely, indirectly; however the influence, absorbed in adolescence or even in childhood, would seem to be far behind us" (305).

Oates's commentary is certainly true for probably the most important writer of the contemporary Gothic story, Stephen King. Like many of the other American authors mentioned in this survey, King discovered Poe when he was in grammar school and he played a part in teaching him how and what to write (Underwood and Miller, 116). In fact, Poe's presence haunts Stephen King's fictional landscape. Whether used to inspire analogous plot and character situations or employed to establish ultimate contrasts, over the past three decades Poe's work has enriched and shaped King's canon. This is evident both in terms of the frequency of direct citations to various Poe works and in the resonance of meaning that Poe has supplied King's fiction. "The Raven" has found its way into several King texts; its themes of isolation and loss reverberate throughout the novel *Gerald's Game* to underscore the situation and disturbed consciousness of the novel's main character. Similarly, the short story "Dolan's Cadillac" addresses the same issue that informs "The Cask of Amontillado": the urge for revenge becomes as much a marker for King's central protagonist as it is for Poe's Montressor. The male characters are compelled to return to the details of their stories, and each is somehow comforted in the retelling of it. Furthermore, the employment of a first-person narration in both tales forces the reader to participate vicariously in the act of revenge. As we are made to witness each brick stacked into the wall of "Amontillado," in King's narrative we are likewise drawn into the main protagonist's obsessional preparations for the live burial of his adversary.

The language "Unmask!" and "The Red Death held illimitable dominion over all" (490) from Poe's "Masque of the Red Death" is repeated throughout *The Shining*. Poe's Prince Prospero has much in common with King's Jack Torrance. They are both supremely selfish men consumed with their own worldly success and social status. And each man inhabits an exclusive party world insulated by wealth and power. In this novel, King not only shares Poe's psychological orientation toward character, he also inherited the latter's awareness of a psychology of place. The Overlook Hotel is animated with the same supernatural biology that we find in Poe's House of Usher and the ever transforming physical environments of "The Pit and the Pendulum" and "William Wilson." From Poe, King learned how to animate a Gothic landscape with a terrible potency that appears to dwarf the vulnerable humans who are held within its bondage. Like Poe's buildings, King's architecture is imbued with a life of its own, an unnatural biology that reflects both the character and history of its former inhabitants. *The Shining's* Overlook Hotel is the ultimate embodiment of the haunted house formula as it was first established in the European Gothic castle and later embellished in Poe's American landscape.

INTERNATIONAL POE: THE MULTIMEDIA LEGACY

While Poe may not have been sufficiently appreciated—financially and artistically—during his lifetime, since his death the world has more than compensated for this unfortunate oversight. One of the more impressive aspects of Poe's literary legacy is its enormous breadth of influence on generations of dance choreographers, filmmakers, musicians, and visual artists that followed him. In music, for instance, Poe's aesthetic left lasting impressions upon classical as well as popular composers. Claude Debussy, regarded as a leader of the ultramodern school of music in nineteenth-century France, wrote two operas based upon Poe stories, while Alan Parsons, who, with the assistance of two hundred musicians, several electronic synthesizers, and the rock group "The Allan Parsons Project," produced an album entitled *Tales of Mystery and Imagination*. Parsons's collection consists of instrumental performances of several Poe stories and poems. In most instances, the "voice" of the narrator, who utters lines directly from Poe's texts, is not really a human voice at all, but rather the simulated language of a moot synthesizer. More recently, several popular Hollywood actors and rock and blues singers produced a collection of readings and song adaptations entitled *Closed on Account of Rabies: Tales and Poems of Edgar Allan Poe*; among the artists contributing to this recording are Christopher Walken reading "The Raven," Marianne Faithfull reciting "Alone," and Deborah Harry (lead singer of the rock group "Blondie") performing a jazz rendition of "The City and the Sea."

Perhaps Poe's influence on musicians through the years can be attributed to the inherently musical quality of his poetry and prose. Poe was always conscious of the rhythmic potential available in the sounds of language and the juxtaposition of certain words at crucial points in a poem or a prose narrative. In "The Poetic Principle," for example, Poe insists that the sole purpose of a poem, its aesthetic essence, ought to be "the *Rhythmical Creation of Beauty*" (1438). In another essay, "The Rationale of Verse," he similarly argues that "in the construction of verse, *melody* should never be left out of view" (1389). As will be demonstrated through specific examples in the next chapter, Poe understood that poetry and music shared the same evocative capabilities, that mood and the manipulation of emotion should be integral to the meaning of a work of art. But it was not just in his poetry that Poe inspired musical analogs. Even his narrative prose demonstrates an omnipresent awareness of cadence and rhythmical patterns within the juxtaposition of words in a sentence. One can hear these qualities in the following passage from the short story "Berenice":

"There is, however, a remembrance of aerial forms—of spiritual and meaning eyes—of sounds, musical yet sad—a remembrance which will not be excluded; a memory like a shadow, vague, variable, indefinite, unsteady" (225). Sometimes Poe's syntax appears too heavily weighted: he seems to be struggling to put too much of everything within a single sentence. One explanation for his distinctive style, however, is the writer's conscious effort to manipulate the imagination of the reader—to take him or her into a realm that never was and perhaps never could be—by detailing the visual perimeters of a room or the musical affiliations inherent in the language of romantic recollection.

What is perhaps equally as surprising as Poe's importance to musicians is his place among visual artists. Few people are aware that the famous painter, Vincent Van Gogh, was a great admirer of Poe's tales and poems. In addition to a reading knowledge of Poe gleaned through his many French translators, Van Gogh drew several pen and ink and charcoal sketches depicting themes undoubtedly influenced by the American, including "The Skull" and several versions of "Death and the Maiden." But it was really Van Gogh's artistic contemporaries who were most influenced by Poe's work, particularly the Symbolists. In his Tahitian memoir *Noa Noa*, Paul Gauguin attributed the inspiration for his painting "Woman with Flower" to Poe's tale "Ligeia." Painters such as Gustave Moreau, Fernand Khnopff, Aubrey Beardsley, Dante Gabriel Rossetti, Odilon Redon, and their fin de siècle brethren who were obsessed with depicting death-haunted images and visions of opulent decadence and the macabre show further evidence of Poe's legacy. Poe essentially influenced the Symbolist imagination in two major ways: he originated the images of drowned people and crumbling edifices shimmering in silver reflections from within stagnant pools of water that are often referenced in Symbolist work, and he evoked an atmosphere of suffocating vegetation and overpowering odors that are, for example, represented in many of the paintings by Degouve de Nunques and Levey-Dhurmer (Jullian, 16). By the end of the nineteenth century, Poe's work found its way into illustrations by Gustave Doré and Henri Matisse. Edouard Manet, the French Impressionist, drew several pen and ink illustrations for Mallarmé's 1875 French translation of "The Raven."

Poe continued to inflame the imaginations of visual artists all through the twentieth century—from the haunted Surrealist dreamscapes of the 1920s to the paintings of Balthasar Klossowski (a.k.a. Balthus), one of the great loners of contemporary art who has made fear and desire as palpable as the oils on his canvases. In Japan, Poe inspired a generation of computer artists and popular illustrators during the 1970s, 1980s, and 1990s who designed video games, computer graphics, and comic books depicting variations on many of Poe's themes, particularly the anxiety-ridden urban man who speeds steadily to his own mental and physical exhaustion.

One of Poe's most intriguing legacies is found in the shadow that he continues to cast over the cinemagraphic arts, perhaps the most powerful medium of the modern world. Poe's entire canon is ideally suited for larger-than-life projection and the surreal possibilities of film. When Poe asserts in "The Philosophy of Composition" that the ultimate purpose of art is to "produce continuously novel effects" (1377), he could just as easily be describing the goal of a Hollywood director. Alfred Hitchcock, arguably the greatest director of modern horror films, read widely and fondly in Poe's fiction. *Strangers on a Train*, *Dial M for Murder*, *Psycho*, *Rear Window*, *Vertigo*, and *The Birds* parallel Poe's own fascination with subliminal projection, body doubles, the art of detection, unholy burials, cryptic murders, resurrected corpses, and the dissolution of the mind's control over itself as a consequence of the intrusion of madness. The Hitchcock hero, like the male protagonist in Poe's tales and poems, typically lives in a self-enclosed universe of his own making, a place that is at once both heaven and hell, protection and prison, as contrived and personal as a dark night's dream. Against this backdrop, human motivations and natural occurrences often become so contradictory that they are ultimately inexplicable. Why the murderer in "The Tell-Tale Heart" kills the old man he professes to love makes no more sense than any rationale used to explain the assault of the birds throughout Hitchcock's 1963 film. Poe and Hitchcock take us into highly individualized and darkly psychological realms that derive their disturbing power from the absolute collapse of conventional reason and predictability.

Over the ensuing decades, work of other Gothic *auteurs*, such as Roman Polanski, David Cronenberg, George Romero, David Fincher, Brian De Palma, and Quentin Tarantino, evince their homage to both Hitchcock and Poe as they push the latter's cinematic fascination with blood and gore to extremes that challenge the very boundaries of special effect technology as well as the tolerance level of audiences. In the films of these contemporary directors, Poe's propensity for visceral violence, exaggeration, and the grotesque—expecially evident in tales such "King Pest" and "The Facts in the Case of M. Valdemar"—is fully realized and often spectacularly surpassed.

The number of horror films professing to be based on stories by Poe is large indeed, but those that remain faithful to their original sources are precious few. Poe's work has always been attractive to filmmakers, in part because it relies so heavily upon visual elements, but also because the narratives remain in the public domain and their copyrights are available without fees or royalties. One of the best film adaptations from Poe's canon is a silent era production by Jean Epstein, an impressive black and white *The Fall of the House of Usher* released in 1928 that illustrates the attraction Poe and the horror genre in general held for the Surrealist movement. "The Tell-Tale Heart" and "Murders in the Rue Morgue" were also early cinematic renditions. Bela Lugosi, most remembered for his starring role in *Dracula*, and Boris Karloff, who played one of the first and still most famous of Hollywood's Frankenstein monsters, also acted in Poe adaptations: Lugosi in *Murders in the Rue Morgue* (1932) and both actors in *The Raven* (1963).

In the early 1960s, American International Pictures produced five films based upon Poe's most popular horror tales, all directed by Roger Corman and centering upon the flamboyant personality of Vincent Price as the melancholic Poe protagonist. Although modestly budgeted (produced and marketed primarily for drive-ins) and prone to outrageous liberties with Poe's original plotlines, these movies were at least true to Poe's fascination with the Gothic phantasmagoria of sensory exaggeration. Perhaps the best of Corman's adaptations is one of the last, *The Masque of the Red Death* (1964). Corman's film does a remarkable job of capturing Prospero's tyrannical and hyperbolic nature. The group of party guests that Prospero has assembled with him inside the sequestered castle wear elaborate costumes, give free reign to their sensual decadence, and perform a tightly choreographed danse macabre at the end of the film that is an appropriate approximation to what Poe names "the sudden impulses of despair or of frenzy from within" (485). More recently, Poe has been again translated into film in two other adaptations, *The Black Cat*, directed by Rob Green, and *The Cask of Amontillado*, directed by Mario Cavalli.

THE PEOPLE'S POE

No other American artist, with the possible exceptions of Mark Twain and perhaps the director Steven Spielberg, have managed to bridge the gap between popular culture and highbrow art to the degree that Poe inspires. He stands simultaneously as a figure at the center of Modernism—the line that stretches from Baudelaire and the Symbolist movement to T.S. Eliot and the rise of New Criticism—and as the inventor or innovator of several popular genres, including science fiction, the detective story, and the horror tale.

Edgar Allan Poe is one of those few artists whose fame has somehow managed to transcend the realm of art itself. His melancholic face is immediately recognizable when it stares out from ceramic coffee mugs, shirts, and shopping bags from Barnes and Noble bookstores. People who do not consider themselves serious readers still acknowledge the name Edgar Allan Poe and at least some of the work he authored. Even "The Raven," a perennial favorite among school children forced to memorize a poem for class recitation, has now been fully immortalized by popular culture in an unforgettable episode of *The Simpsons*.

Poe is at once a tremendously significant literary icon and a refugee from a salacious Halloween costume party. He may have been the first American writer to be embraced by the many important international artists examined throughout this chapter, but he is also the progenitor of a line that includes a whole genre of Hollywood B-grade horror films that have gone directly from screening room to late-night television cable and video cassette. Each week the newspapers herald the release of a new book or film that explores the bizarre, the mysterious, or the supernatural. An obsession with the fantastic and all things Gothic occupies a central place in popular culture. As the critic Mark Edmundson has persuasively insisted, "1990s Gothic modes are beholden to the genius of American terror, to Edgar Allan Poe. Poe's . . . spirit, like a specter from one of his own tales, has risen up to brood over the *fin de siècle*" (71).

Indeed, Poe might have felt much more at home in our contemporary epoch than he ever was in his own. He would have witnessed his vision of life treated not as aberration but as reality; he would have found his poetic embrace of surreal worlds and his literary propensity for perverse pleasure translated into street fashions, advertisements, discussions of sexuality, video games, record lyrics and cover designs, magazine art, and Internet websites. Even the evening news underscores a daily fascination with Poe-esque violence and carnage. It is no longer possible to witness the events of one of these televised programs without encountering the sense that we ought indeed to be very much afraid—of our neighbors, certainly, but also of ourselves. In its fascination with all things Gothic, our age continually references the very pathology Poe once described, as the serial killer has emerged from police blotters and psychological profiles to become an emblem of our cultural moment. The Jeffrey Dahmers and Charles Mansons have inspired the Hannibal Lecters and John Does (the killer in the film *Seven*) of contemporary film and fiction. There is an unmistakable line of connection between Poe's murderers, whose bloody crimes have resulted in the narrating of personal histories from condemned prison cells and asylums, and the powerful, highly intelligent, and utterly deranged killers who stalk our streets as well as our movie and television screens.

For the last few years of his life, Poe chose to dress exclusively in black, even during the most humid summer weather in Virginia and South Carolina. He was the first real American Gothic—a person who would have felt comfortable with contemporary urban teenage goths who listen to the music of Nine Inch Nails and German "techno-industrial noise" while employing excessive amounts of black eyeliner to exaggerate their lips and eyes. It has always been my belief that Edgar Allan Poe might have appreciated an evening in their company just as much—and perhaps even more—as one spent with college English professors who have devoted years to studying his life and work.

3

The Art of Poetry

Certainly Poe is best known, and justifiably so, for his short tales, a genre he helped both to perfect and legitimize. Ask most people, students and scholars alike, to identify one or two representative works by Poe and the majority will select "The Tell-Tale Heart," "The Pit and the Pendulum," "The Cask of Amontillado," or even "The Fall of the House of Usher." As a poet, Poe never quite achieved the fame and recognition associated with his prose narratives; even our own age tends to identify him poetically as the author of "The Raven," and not much else. But this was not always the case. As surveyed in the last chapter, in the latter part of the nineteenth century, Poe was internationally known and respected posthumously for his poetry. Perhaps the twentieth century has been less receptive to his verse because it lacks the sharp psychological edge of his tales. Further, the total collection of poems he produced remained small—sixty-three in total. Many of these were composed early in his literary career, when Poe was a neophyte author, and before he fell into financial distress and was forced to write for money.

The majority of his poems can be characterized as short ballads and lyrics— deeply personalized love songs rendered from the perspective of a melancholic male—that are both brief and intensely emotional. Many of the shorter poems are lyrics of irrecoverable loss—loss of love, loss of youth, while longer poems such as "Al Aaraaf" and "The Raven" are versified narratives. The locales of his poems are often idealized sites of beauty or Edens of the imagination. Other poems reveal a deserted psychic terrain that combines elements of beauty and horror within a doomed world viewed in its final moments.

For some readers, Poe's poetry is not worth a second glance. They find it overly derivative, sentimental and redundant in theme, and too technical—that is, obsessed with meter, rhyme, and poetic stylistics. Much of this criticism seems appropriate. All his life Poe studied other poets carefully, modeling his own verse after theirs, and as a consequence it often fails to distinguish itself (as do his greatest short stores) either in terms of original subject matter or in radically inventive forms of expression. In fact, arguably the best and certainly the most famous half dozen or so poems Poe was to produce were written during the last five years of his life.

That said, Poe's poetry is an absolutely critical component to understanding his literary vision. If Poe's most important tales of horror and suspense are dramatic studies of aberrant psychology and the products of human depravity, more than any other genre in which he chose to work, his poetry is the best place to uncover his predilection toward fantasy and the conception of a fantastic literary universe. In short, it is in his verse that Poe, the artist who was fascinated with imaginative worlds that never were and never could be, can best be appreciated. In his best poems, Poe's language revolves around vague and indeterminate subjects; surreal vistas are summoned forth through remarkable sound effects and impressive imagery that place the reader in irrational, death-haunted, and dreamlike realms. Poe the poet is always reminding us of just how strange it is to be human and the levels in which the mind—particularly through the faculty of memory—can be induced to revel in this strangeness.

"SONNET—TO SCIENCE" (1829)

One of Poe's earliest poems, this first appeared in the book that launched his literary career, *Al Aaraaf, Tamerlane, and Minor Poems,* in December 1829. The poem was used as an introduction to the entire collection.

SETTING AND PLOT

The sonnet is a direct address to nineteenth-century science as an emerging worldview. As such, it is a romantic protest against the discipline's tendency to reduce the mysteries of the universe to empirical evidence and rational explanations. In contrast to the romantic artist—who relies upon myth, magic, and mystical revelation—the scientist looks for supportable evidence to explain the workings of the world through hypotheses which, in turn, if judged highly probable, are raised to the status of theories. And further, instead of viewing science as merely an alternative to magic and mystery, scientists seek to supplant and even destroy these latter elements in their relentless pursuit of "provable knowledge." In contrast to those romantic individuals who "seek for treasure in the jewelled skies" (38), the scientist's "peering eyes" drain spiritual energy out of even the most vital experience by subjecting it to overanalysis and reason. Even the poet's authority has been undermined, and it is this fact that most incites Poe's wrath: "Why preyest thou thus upon the poet's heart,/ Vulture, whose wings are dull realities" (38). All of nature stands in terror of what science is capable of doing to it; even the formidable and ancient powers of the goddess Diana are challenged, while mythological wood nymphs must "seek shelter in some happier star" (38).

SYMBOLS AND THEMES

Poe does not even attempt to render a balanced argument in this critique of science (an inherently neutral and apolitical construct). His generalizations about the entire discipline, for example, make it impossible to see the beauty inherent in a scientific explanation or to recognize that there are conflicting scientific theories that can often render the discipline anything but "dull." Indeed, there is an artistic talent in generating a good hypothesis—for example, Einstein's theory of relativity—that is the equal to any poem in terms of observing and appreciating life experience or asking questions about why things are the way they are. For those students who identify exclusively with the humanities, however, this sonnet does little by way of modifying the view that science and scientists strip the joy out of living.

Poe the romantic adheres to negative stereotypes all through this verse; in his eyes, science is the purest enemy of the imagination. His employment of verbs such as "dragged," "driven," and "torn" go on to highlight the aggressive and intrusive nature of rationalism in Western culture. The poet has no place for such intrusions in his work since they stand directly in the flight path of the winged muse. Like the goddess Diana and the mythic wood nymphs that Poe places under assault in this sonnet, the poet himself feels displaced by the encroaching philosophy of science. And while the poem may not be a convincing renunciation of the scientific method, it does serve as a prophetic anticipation of the misuse of science that would come to besiege not only Poe's generation but those to follow. Although we seldom think of Edgar Allan Poe as an antitechnological environmentalist, surely our own time has seen ample evidence—in nuclear energy and biological weaponry, to name only two examples—of what happens when science is manipulated and abused by individual scientists bereft of scruples as well as poetic vision.

"THE CITY IN THE SEA" (1845)

Although it was first published under this title in 1845, earlier versions of this poem had appeared as early as 1831 under different titles. Poe's fantasy is one of his most romantic poems and was much admired by the English Pre-Raphaelite poets and the French Symbolists. Its underwater landscape closely resembles the ethereal realm of Jules Verne's *Journey to the Center of the Earth*, a novel that was strongly influenced by several of Poe's fantastic voyages, including this particular poem.

SETTING AND PLOT

"The City in the Sea" is an excellent illustration of Poe's interest in creating imaginative worlds unto themselves where organic life forms neither live nor reproduce. Like "Dream-Land" and "The Valley of Unrest," poems that closely resemble "City" in atmospheric ambiance, these are haunted and deserted dreamscapes that exist without air or movement. In fact, the only "action" that occurs in this poem appears to be in the presence of light, the illuminated glow of hellfire emanating from below the city that provides: "The waves now a redder glow" (68).

Perhaps a version of the lost Atlantis or maybe a future vision of a coastal city such as Venice, Italy, its "shrines and places and towers" finally submerged beneath "melancholy waters" (67), this is a fantastic vista where death and ruin reign. Poe paints a dark portrait of an ancient abandoned city whose magnificent buildings and towers suggest that it was once a thriving metropolis. Now, however, it is no longer the City of God, the heavenly city extolled by Augustine and other philosophers, but an extension of hell itself. There are no human beings left to populate this eerie place, only the shadows of their past presence. As such, there really is no plot nor action to this poem; it relies almost exclusively on its atmospheric setting to create a bizarre other-worldliness where death triumphs over all things human: "While from a proud tower in the town/ Death looks gigantically down" (67).

SYMBOLS AND THEMES

"The City in the Sea" is a good illustration of Poe's employing fantastic imagery and convoluted sounds in his poetry to create a vision of the macabre. Like a dream hallucination or the landscape of a dystopian science-fiction film (e.g., *Mad Max's Beyond Thunderdome*), Poe imagines an entire city where decrepit buildings hold themselves together, where there is no physical movement, human presence, or even an awareness of time. The whole place appears to "float pendulous in air," as if suspended in a vacuum. If the reader has ever walked the streets of a city late at night during a serious snowstorm, perhaps this sense of urban abandonment is close to what Poe sought to invoke through the language and imagery of this poem. There is certainly a sense of strangeness in this work, but perhaps Poe's truest intention here was to represent the ultimate void of death. In crossing from one world to another, a landscape that was once comprehensible and rational is transformed into something vaguely mystifying and mysterious. And, as is often the case in Poe, the reader is at least as attracted to this monstrous manifestation of a craving for the shadow of death as he is repulsed by its very desolation.

"THE RAVEN" (1845)

Without qualification, this is Poe's most famous poem. Subsequent printings and public performances of the poem throughout Poe's lifetime were numerous. In fact, on almost every occasion where Poe delivered a public reading or lecture, the audience fully expected him to conclude with a recitation of "The Raven." The poem is almost synonymous with the name of Poe and was often the subject of his own critical commentaries on the art of poetry, especially "The Philosophy of Composition" (see the "Alternate Reading" section at the end of this chapter). In fact, Poe was sometimes called "The Raven" as a nickname. The poem is essentially a nocturnal dialogue between a bereaved lover and an intrusive raven who visits him, apparently to intensify the misery of the narrator as it refuses the poet's command to "leave my loneliness unbroken!—quit the bust above my door!" (86). A conversation ensues between poet and bird with each of the mourner's frustrated queries provoking a single word response: "Nevermore."

SETTING AND PLOT

At midnight of a bleak night in December, the grieving lover-narrator-poet sits alone in his dreary chamber reading books in an effort to avoid thinking about his "lost Lenore." His strategy backfires, however, as his overly conscious attempt to escape her memory only serves to summon it. Upon hearing a tapping at his chamber door, the narrator allows a "stately" raven to fly into the chamber through an open window, whereupon the bird proceeds to perch on a bust of Pallas above the door. At first, the bird brings the grieving lover a degree of distraction, beguiling him into a smile when he asks the bird its name. But it quickly becomes apparent that this raven is not present for the poet's amusement; in fact, quite the contrary, as its mindless repetition of the word "Nevermore" to each of the narrator's questions creates an ever more frustrating and irritating situation. The poet questions the bird at first about Lenore's whereabouts, then wonders if he will reencounter her in the afterlife, and finally if the narrator himself will ever find peace in her absence. To each of these questions the bird's consistent reply infuriates him at the same time as it deepens his sense of loss. Real raven or hallucination, good or evil, bird or demon—it is never confirmed exactly what this intrusive raven represents, but what is clear is that the bird helps to reveal a human mind that is unraveling, and that finally gives up its hold on sanity and descends completely into the madness of despair. At the end of the poem, the reader is informed that the raven is still present in the chamber of the narrator and that the poet's soul will never escape the shadow of the bird.

SYMBOLS

In the course of the poem, it is clear that the role of the raven quickly changes from one of amusement to something more somber. Dating back to Homer, the raven has always been a bad omen. As the poet realizes this fact, his attitude toward the bird changes from one of bemusement to irritation and ultimate despair. The raven has come to him with a prophetic message of negation: his lover will not be coming back, the prospect of reuniting with her at a future time and place is unlikely, and the poet's personal loss and loneliness will not be soon relieved. The bird perched above his door, unable—or at least unwilling—to do anything more than croak the same negative refrain, becomes an apt symbol of the narrator's impotent state of being.

THEMES

In the short story "The Imp of the Perverse," Poe posits that human beings, despite their best efforts at self-preservation, also possess a counterbalancing urge toward self-torture and even self-destruction: "[I]n the case of that something which I term *perverseness*, the desire to be well is not only not aroused, but a strongly antagonistical sentiment exists" (828). This principle of perverseness is illustrated in many of Poe's short stories, most notably "The Tell-Tale Heart" and "The Black Cat." The poem "The Raven" is most obviously about a lost love and the narrator's inability, or unwillingness, to shed his romantic melancholia. Poe's speaker subsists inside a room where he perversely studies and covets his pain; his isolation is interrupted by the raven, whose sole purpose centers upon increasing the narrator's misery. But note that the narrator does nothing to force the bird into leaving—he never does call for help from a pest exterminator—and his questions regarding the ultimate destiny of the dead Lenore are rhetorically constructed to end in the bird's negative comment. As the bird is allowed to remain in the room, essentially stimulating the poet's sense of despair, we realize that its presence parallels the man's own desire to nurture his grief. Like the forsaken lover who continues to drive by his girlfriend's house even after she has dumped him for a new boyfriend, Poe's narrator clings with a desperate zeal to his grief; it is all he has left. Poe argues that there is a certain secreted, delicious pain, like picking at a scab, that comes from such examples of perversity. At the conclusion of the poem, we are to believe that the raven has become a permanent resident of the poet's chamber and soul; moreover, that the narrator appears to gain a real pleasure in the additional gloom afforded by the raven's presence: "And my soul from out that shadow that lies floating on the floor/ Shall be lifted—nevermore!" (86).

"ULALUME: A BALLAD" (1847)

A ten-stanza version of this poem was first printed unsigned in December 1847. It was later reprinted with its last stanza omitted in 1848. The name "Ulalume" refers to a fictional beloved who, like Lenore and Annabel Lee, has died mysteriously and is currently mourned by an isolated male. The name probably was chosen by Poe for its lyrical phonics that variously suggest "ululation" (to wail or lament loudly), "luna" (moon), "undulate" (a rising and falling to either side), or perhaps even "illuminate" (to enlighten intellectually or spiritually).

SETTING AND PLOT

Typical of a Poe work, the poem is set in a dark and dreary dream-like realm, occurring in "the lonesome October" through "the ghoul-haunted woodland of Weir" (89). As in "The Fall of the House of Usher," there is a swamp, a misty landscape, and an atmosphere that is suggestive of dissolution and decay. Through this forsaken landscape the poet-narrator takes an autumnal stroll with Psyche, his soul. The purpose of the journey is not clear at first, even to the narrator himself, but it bears some kind of connection to his beloved Ulalume, who died exactly one year ago to the day: "Ah, night of all nights in the year!" (89). The poet and his soul both distrust this forlorn place to which they have wandered, although it is not until the end of the ballad, when the narrator arrives at the door of a "legended tomb," that he recalls it was exactly one year ago he "brought a dread burden down here" (91) for internment. The poem ends with a question: [W]hat demon, or spiritual agency, estranged from both God and man, has brought the poet back to this place to "tempt me here" (91)?

SYMBOLS

While making this journey, the poet reveals to his soul—Psyche—that he is drawn to the crescent moon goddess Astarte, an ancient Near Eastern symbol of sexual fertility and carnal passion. We are informed that the narrator exists in a "volcanic" (89) state, as his sensual passions have been aroused. Psyche grows apprehensive and warns the narrator, " 'Sadly this star I mistrust' " (90). Psyche would have the poet resist the attractions of the flesh symbolically represented by Astarte and focus his energies instead upon remaining true to Ulalume, symbol of the poet's muse, or true spiritual legacy. Upon recognizing that he has traveled unwittingly to "the vault of the lost Ulalume!" (90), the narrator experiences a kind of dark epiphany and grasps fully the choice between remembrance and forgetfulness, as well as between the love of flesh and the love of spirit. His higher self now reactivated, he resists the temptations that have emerged from unconscious motivations and consciously reasserts his will toward self-discipline.

The poem is, at least on one level of interpretation, a symbolic struggle between the Freudian id and superego (see the "Alternative Reading" section at the end of chapter 5), or the poet's conscious understanding versus his unconscious urges. Motivated by his desire for pleasure, the poem is a symbolic descent into the poet's unconscious, where he is pulled by the urge to forget the past and engage sensual experience (Astarte) in the present. But Psyche, or the ever attentive superego of the poet, creates a crisis within the self in arguing against such a course of action. The soul insists that the poet maintain his focus and resist the temptations of the id, holding faithful to Ulalume's symbol of spiritual essence. Rescued from destruction by the warning of his superego, the poet leaves this decadent place with his virtue intact.

THEMES

Although Poe the poet despised allegory as a poetic form, he may well have evinced in "Ulalume" some insight into the struggle he underwent after Virginia's death over whether he should seek the companionship of new women (Sarah Helen Whitman and Elmira Roister) or remain chaste and true to Virginia's memory, who died less than a year before "Ulalume" was written. It is, after all, a part of the poet himself—his own soul—that guides him to his true love and then insists that he remain faithful to the past he shared with her. As if in keeping with this final choice, the poem ends with the poet and Psyche acknowledging that the journey is now over—"bar up our way and to ban it" (91)—and that the crisis of self symbolized in the poem's conflict between flesh and spirit is likewise concluded.

"THE BELLS" (1849)

Although this ode was written in 1848, it was not published until after Poe's death in December 1849. The poem underwent at least three revisions, each one growing in length as Poe added additional lines to each of the four sections.

SETTING AND PLOT

The poem is cast in the form of an irregular ode—that is, separate sections similar to each other in terms of central concepts and general poetic form, but also different as the sections vary from one another in length and purpose. "The Bells" is divided into four sections or movements, each of which enjoins the reader through onomatopoeic devices to attend to the different variances of the bells's language. This poem of course was written before the advent of modern technology, when bells were employed in a variety of specialized circumstances, some of which are no longer used—for example, as an alarm system for waking a town besieged by fire, or even the more attractive sounds of bells employed to signal the approach of a horse-drawn sleigh.

In the first section, the winter sleigh bells sound "silver" as they "tinkle/ In the icy air of night" (92). As we might imagine, the sound these bells make is light and frothy, "a crystalline delight" (92) that is meant to signal the merriment of a nocturnal sleigh ride. In the second section, the golden bells associated with a wedding ring out in the spring or summer "[t]hrough the balmy air of night" (92). Perhaps not as superficially light as the silver notes of sleigh bells but still nonetheless euphoric, the wedding bells produce a slightly more serious tone as Poe chooses to emphasize their connection to the future harmony of a married couple: "How it dwells/ On the Future!—how it tells/ Of the rapture that impels" (93). In the third part, the bells change their tone completely, shattering the pleasant atmospheres evoked in the first and second sections, as the "startled ear of Night" (93) is ripped apart by the "shriek" of bells that call attention to a "frantic fire" (93). The alarm bells ring with a "clamorous appeal"; the violent intensity of their sound, sharply opposed to the gentle "molten-golden notes/ And all in tune" associated with the wedding bells, is meant to suggest the "mad expostulation" of a fire raging out of control. And finally, in contrast to the freneticism of these fire bells, the last section of the poem features bells that are constructed of heavy iron, and the slow toll of their weightiness underscores the solemn mood of a funeral. While the fire bell section is written and meant to be read with a deliberate quality of breathlessness—individual words strung together in such a way that they appear nearly to tumble over one another—Poe's change in diction and rhythm in this final section is a conscious effort to slow the poem down. The joy and sweetness evoked in the first two sections, and the intense anxiety of the fire bells in the third, are completely abandoned in the sonorous, nearly languid melancholia of the fourth: "For every sound that floats/ From the rust within their throats/ Is a groan" (94).

SYMBOLS

The poem is an interesting variation on the poetic device called personification, the act of providing human qualities or characteristics to inanimate objects or animals. By themselves, of course, metal bells are neither happy nor sad; human beings supply their sounds with an interpretative meaning. The different types and corresponding sounds produced by the respective bells used in each of the four sections symbolize distinct human variances in mood and attitude. From the joyous ringing of the sleigh bell, to the rapturous cry of wedding bells, to the terror associated with a bell used to summon help, to the sadness aligned with a funeral—Poe's bells are kept tinkling, throbbing, moaning, groaning, and dancing according to the human mood that resonates with its own unique voice.

THEMES

As discussed at greater length in the "Alternative Reading" section at the end of this chapter, Poe maintained very definite attitudes regarding the purpose, unity, proportion, and construction of poetry. Since he always sought to create a close association between music and poetic language, sound and rhythm are crucial elements in all his poems. "The Bells" may well be the best illustration of their usage, as each section relies heavily upon alliteration, alternating interior rhythms, assonantal rhyme (the repetition of identical or similar vowel sounds, especially in stressed syllables, with changes in the intervening consonants), and monosyllabic rhyme to produce a different musical effect. Several of the individual lines contain alliterating consonants that fashion a verbal melody appropriate to the theme of the section. When producing the atmospheric effect of the golden wedding bells, for example, a kind of linguistical euphoria can be heard in the lines: "Oh, from out the sounding cells/ What a gush of euphony voluminously wells!" (93). The repeated hard "s" sounds in the words "sounding" and "cells" that come at the end of the first line are neatly balanced by the hard "v" and "w" sounds that appear at the end of the following line. All of this is employed by the poet in the second section to create a feeling or suggestion of the hard ring of the bells themselves, as if someone were shaking them with great enthusiasm at the moment a newly married couple departs their wedding chapel.

"The Bells" is an auditory delight. While many poets are interested in evoking the musical elements inherent in artfully constructed lyrical diction, there are few works that succeed in doing so with the virtuosity of Poe's poem. Perhaps what links "The Bells" to other Poe verse, such as "The Raven" and "The City in the Sea," is the creation of a certain atmosphere that stimulates the senses more than the intellect. Poe's poetic images and sounds evoke a deeply haunting quality that is less the result of deliberate consideration on the part of the reader than a more spontaneous reliance on sense awareness and feelings.

"ANNABEL LEE" (1849)

This famous recitative set piece is Poe's final finished poem, composed in May 1849 and published posthumously several months later. Various women in Poe's life, including Sarah Anna Lewis, Helen Whitman, and Elmira Shelton, saw themselves in the poem's child heroine, but the poem is clearly a keepsake for Virginia Clemm Poe, who died two years before its creation.

SETTING AND PLOT

Many years ago in a kingdom by the sea, the narrator-poet informs us that he was in love with a woman named Annabel Lee. Their lives together were simple: "she lived with no other thought/ Than to love and be loved by me" (102). Their love was so pure and virtuous that even "the winged seraphs of Heaven/ Coveted her and me" (102). For some unexplained reason, perhaps the jealousy of God and the angels, Annabel Lee dies suddenly, her kinsmen take her body away from the poet and bury her in a place near the sea, leaving the narrator alone in his grief. The narrator concludes that their love—stronger than "those older than we" (103) and even the envious angels—continues to endure, and that the soul of the poet and his Annabel Lee remain joined, defying death.

SYMBOLS

Annabel Lee is one of the great symbols of romantic love. The woman in this poem is both Virginia Poe, the poet's wife who died from tuberculosis in Poe's presence, and a symbol of idealized love. Closely aligned to the concept of beauty in Poe's poetic universe, the poem celebrates the love shared between youth who may not possess the wisdom of experience, but more than make up for this in the passion of their feelings. The poem extols the superiority of the child-lover over the rational adult.

THEMES

"Annabel Lee" lyricizes thematic issues common to many of Poe's works: the death of a beautiful woman, her interment, and the poet's undying love and de-ification of her memory. Poe's lifelong resentment of paternal authority may be heard in the lines: "So that her highborn kinsmen came and bore her away from me" (102).

"Annabel Lee" most resembles "The Raven" insofar as both poems are told from the point of view of a narrator who has recently lost an important woman in his life, both poems exist not so much as narrative actions but as evocations of feelings, and both lament the chasm that exists between romantic love and reality. As in "The Raven," the poet clings stubbornly to the memory of his idealized lost love in spite of the fact that this love is doomed. Perhaps the only place where the two poems diverge thematically is over the issue of degree of separation. Annabel Lee endures as an ever constant evocation for the poet of this poem; he remains willingly connected to her in spite of her physical absence. In "The Raven," on the other hand, the bird is there as an ever present reminder of the *barriers* currently separating the poet from the lost Lenore; Lenore's memory eventually becomes less a permanent symbol of idealized beauty and love than a constant source of pain and personal negation.

ALTERNATE READING: GENRE CRITICISM

Literary criticism has been in existence for centuries. In fact, one might argue that once the first literary texts were written down by their creators, certain readers who were also writers—or critics—felt the need to explain and evaluate what these texts meant. Literary critics ask basic questions concerning the philosophical, psychological, aesthetic, and structural meanings of the text itself. The separation of literature into different genres is a way of categorizing a certain type or style of writing. In genre scholarship, a critic seeks to gain deeper insight into a writer's use of a specific type or category of artistic composition as it is marked by a distinctive style, form, or content. For example, if a literary critic were interested in pursuing a genre analysis of the short story, issues such as how a fiction writer tends to employ narrative plotting, environment and setting, or the recurring role of similar fictional personalities might be of notable importance. Genre criticism helps readers to understand the contributions authors make toward exploring and sometimes even advancing the specific literary genre(s) in which they have chosen to work. In other words, how an individual author applies or alters the conventions generally associated with a recognized literary form is an issue worthy of study. While it is true that not all writers advance the literary genre to which their contributions belong, each artist uses certain aspects or conventions of the genre for his or her own purposes. And in some rare instances, an author emerges to transform an entire genre.

Poe saw himself as a genre innovator—and, remarkably enough, in several of the different literary forms he employed during the course of his career. Poe was the consummate "utility infielder": he could play nearly every position and play it well. He did more than any other writer before him to explain the conventions of what governs a short story, or how the length and particular form of a poem added to its overall effect. His pronouncements on the significance of unity in a given literary work anticipated the formalist movement by almost an entire century. Certainly one of Poe's greatest contributions to literary history remains a collection of essays that he composed late in his career defining the most significant themes and structures that he felt were central to an understanding of the genre of poetry. In a trio of essays—"The Philosophy of Composition" (1846), "The Rationale of Verse" (1848), and "The Poetic Principle" (1850)—the writer articulated and demonstrated his theories on the ideal nature of poetry. And while some of his tenets, such as the core argument that "the death of a beautiful woman is, unquestionably, the most poetic topic in the world" (1379), may strike some readers as misogynistic or perhaps a little warped, the intellectually rigorous and idiosyncratic nature of Poe's ruminations are precisely what make them valuable to students and scholars studying his work. His literary criticism provides startling insights into his own creative endeavors.

For the moment, let us return to this famous statement regarding poetry and the death of women. The central themes of "The Raven," "Annabel Lee," "Ulalume," and "Lenore," among others, pivot around Poe's association of a beautiful woman and her death. Moreover, all these poems contemplate this condition from the point of view of a bereaved lover, whom Poe trusts to possess "the lips best suited for such [a] topic" (1379). Now while it is clear that this subject haunted Poe personally, a consequence of his own biographical tragedies, it is also important to note that Poe wished to create a poetry of feeling, to put the reader in a situation where she would be forced to identify with the experience of bereavement. "Melancholy," he wrote, "is the most legitimate of all the poetical tones" (1377). All of us have experienced either the death or the abandonment of someone we once loved; the recovery process is never easy nor is it often clearly demarcated. Furthermore, in making this loss a beautiful woman, Poe wishes to complicate further our response to this specific loss: that the quality of melancholia is deepened whenever it is associated with the death of a lovely female, that fate is necessarily indifferent to the power of beauty, and that destruction is an essential element of life experience.

On the other hand, Poe discovered a terrible power inherent in the artistic renderings of such destruction. Poe's lovers are consumed in a blaze in which ecstasy and horror are identical. His male survivors, attuned and sensitized by their respective personal tragedies, are in intimate contact with their deepest emotions for perhaps the first time in their lives. They come consequently to savor the exquisite intricacies of their loss because it evokes an intensity of feeling that threatens to overwhelm them. For Poe, the lines separating passion, sex, and pain continually intersected. Such particular aesthetic considerations in his poetry are precisely what inspired an entire international generation of nineteenth-century Symbolist and Decadent poets to recognize in Poe their true artistic progenitor. Like Poe, the Symbolists and Decadents were drawn to an art of strangeness and obsession that deliberately blurred the boundaries of the physical (erotic) and spiritual worlds.

For Poe, the death of a beautiful woman told from the perspective of her abandoned lover created two possibilities that can be seen as crucial elements in his poetic universe: (1) an atmosphere in nature and architecture that conforms to and mirrors the internal sentiments of an individual immersed in grief, and (2) a vehicle for helping to establish a poem's "totality of effect." First, the essence of effect, for Poe, is proportion. All the individual aspects of a poem—from its length, to its refrain, to its subject matter—had to balance proportionately. Without proportion, there could be no unity (totality). Next, a long poem was a contradiction in terms; any poem that was not readable at one sitting relinquished the immediate impact of its sentiments: "[T]he brevity [of a poem] must be in direct ratio of the intensity of the intended effect" (1375). Since, for Poe, the "intended effect" was necessarily melancholic in nature, all the other elements of an individual poem—rhythmic cadence, end rhyme, repetition, and metrical discipline—must underscore the poem's sense of sadness in order to create a unified whole. Finally, the death of a beautiful woman provides the opportunity for creating a self-enclosed world. The reader enters the mind of the narrator-bereaved lover only to find himself trapped in the stifling atmosphere of a funeral home from which there is neither escape nor modulation. And while we come to appreciate this atmosphere as a deathless condition for the narrator, its "totality of effect" is contrarily weakened if the *reader* is forced to remain its prisoner for too long.

While Poe obviously thought long and hard about what elements appropriately constitute the poetic sentiment, he was remarkably consistent about what these elements were. As we have seen, "Beauty," unity, and brevity were core components. An element of the bizarre or strange, even an "exquisite sense of Deformity or disproportion" ("Fifty Suggestions") only added and heightened Poe's appreciation of "Beauty." To enrich these sensibilities, Poe argued that poetry, while inferior to music, must endeavor to approximate its melodies in the rhythmic music of word combinations, repetition, and rhyme. "The Bells" stands out as perhaps the best illustration of Poe's employment of the techniques of music to poetry; the tension and distortion that highlight the differences among the various bells is the real subject of the poem—its form and its music. His other poetry likewise relies heavily upon the careful arrangement of words in proportional balance based upon sound resonances. Poe informs us in "The Philosophy of Composition," for example, that he was quite deliberate in selecting the word "Nevermore" as the refrain for "The Raven." Its melancholic three syllabic monotone resonates perfectly against the despair of the student-narrator. In Poe's aesthetics, the admixture of music and poetry became a core component of beauty: "It is in Music, perhaps, that the soul most nearly attains the great end for which, when inspired with the Poetic Sentiment, it struggles—the creation of supernal Beauty" (1438).

In "The Poetic Principle," Poe maintains that the poetic spirit is not only unified by the proportion and harmony of its individual elements, but that it also infuses other art forms: "The Poetic Sentiment, of course, may develop itself in various modes in Painting, in Sculpture, in Architecture, in the Dance—very especially in Music—and very particularly, and with a wide field, in the composition of the Landscape Garden" (1437). Most readers have no problem seeing the interconnection that exists among poetry, music, art, and dance, but what is particularly interesting in this passage is Poe's inclusion of a landscape garden. It probably should come as no surprise that a collection or garden of shrubs, flowers, and grass trained, pruned, and arranged in a certain artistic pattern would be particularly attractive to the author of poems such as "The City in the Sea," "Ulalume," and "The Valley of Unrest." A landscape garden, as Poe means it here, is a natural outgrowth that is given shape and definition by human hands. Baroque in conception, if not in specific point of origin, the landscape garden resembles nothing so much as the Renaissance poetic game (also popular in the eighteenth century) called shaped verse. The artist, be it poet or gardener, forms the raw material into surprising forms and arrangements, which, one may say, nature never intended it to assume. It is the creation of a world—sometimes crossing over into the realm of the exotic and bizarre because it is so unnatural—unto itself. Like painting or music, the landscape garden is an artistic representation formed by man but then meant to exist apart from our world, nature, the moment itself. Many of Poe's atmospheric poems suggest this same independence from both a recognizable reality and the audience itself. As we have seen, Poe found a particular beauty in the strange and the contrived, but he also wanted poetry to suggest imaginative places where the reader would feel perhaps the same sensation as standing in a landscape garden. He wanted poetry to be an extreme extension of the human imagination rendered into art that exists on its own terms and bears an original form never before appreciated.

Poetry was the great love of Poe's life. But as can be traced all through Poe's personal history, the things and people he loved most were destined to be taken from him. To support himself, and later his wife and aunt/mother-in-law, Poe was forced to focus his prodigious energies toward other, more financially rewarding literary pursuits. And yet, in spite of these necessities, Poe never entirely abandoned his poetic career, as his genre criticism on poetry—most of which was composed late in his career—and the handful of excellent verse he wrote during his final years, more than aptly indicate. Moreover, the importance of the poetic enterprise to Poe—from its reliance upon lyrical metrics and deliberate diction in order to produce desired atmospheric effects to its themes of love's loss and melancholic brooding—cannot be separated from the most enduring features of his prose fiction. In other words, Poe turned to composing prose narratives, editing, and book reviewing primarily to make a living as a writer, but all of these enterprises—both in language usage and choice of subject matter—constantly reveal the hand of the poet. The next chapter, dealing with the vampiric women characters found in Poe's short stories, merely extends and deepens the discussion of romantic love and lethal longing that is central to any discussion of Poe and the art of poetry.

4

Vampiric Love Stories

As traced throughout the preceding chapter, Poe's most memorable poems revolve around the consistent lament of a lover grieving over a recently deceased
wife or girlfriend. The writer likewise produced a series of short, melancholic
love stories that pose remarkable parallels to these poems. Most of these love
stories were written and published in the middle of Poe's career, from about
1835 to 1842, and then revised and reprinted, sometimes more than once, in
newspapers and magazines published in different eastern American cities. Poe
conducted most of his expansive career in magazine publishing, when economic depression and a lack of clearly defined or enforced copyright laws
brought on a demand for cheap publications. Each time one of his tales was reprinted, Poe sometimes received additional payment and expanded his audience base.

Magazine authors were seldom paid for their writing during this era, and,
when paid, usually relinquished complete control over the publication of their
work in exchange for money. Although these love stories would eventually
come to represent some of his most enduring fiction, Poe obtained very little
money for their publication. For example, he appears to have received ten dollars for the first printing of "Ligeia" in the *Baltimore American Museum* in
1838, about fifty cents a page for one of the most important short stories in
Poe's canon, as well as all of nineteenth-century American literature. Occasionally, a contemporary reviewer would make reference to one of these short
stories, but as with most of Poe's work, their true literary value would only be

recognized posthumously. In the erratic publishing world of the 1830s and 1840s, Poe was better known as a critic than as a creative writer. His fiction and poetry were widely dispersed in various magazines and newspapers published on the East Coast, but as a creative artist his reputation was inauspicious; he remained unaffiliated with either a literary genre or a regional locale.

In 1842, Poe asked the famous novelist Charles Dickens to try to use his influence to find an English publisher to reprint his 1839 edition of the *Tales of the Grotesque and Arabesque*, a collection that brought together for the first time many of Poe's love stories in one volume, including "Morella," "Ligeia," and "The Fall of the House of Usher." Dickens promised to help him and tried to do so, but his efforts were in vain. Dickens wrote to Poe, by way of attempted consolation, that "no collection of detached pieces by an unknown writer" would be likely to find an English publisher (Silverman, 1991, 199). The result of this endeavor for Poe was the usual sense of disappointment mixed with resentment, for his rejection in England merely mirrored in very real ways his continued invisibility in the United States. The general unwillingness to value Poe's art during his lifetime became, as Baudelaire would later argue, an important factor in his self-definition as an outsider, making Poe ever more conscious of his literary talent as, if not dispensable, then at least unappreciated by the world.

In poems such as "The Raven," "Ulalume," and "Annabel Lee," Poe's women are strictly relegated to the arena of male recollection; they stay dead. The female subjects of his lyrical verse certainly continue to haunt the respective men in their lives who, in turn, maintain romantic vigils over both their women's tombs and memories. But Lenore, Ulalume, and Annabel Lee never actually make physical appearances in any of the poems that are about them. Poe's prose narratives that deal with the subject of dead and dying women, on the other hand, feature the same melancholic male narrator-lovers found in the poetry, but the female objects of their affection are no longer permanently disposed to the crypt. Not content merely to haunt the psyches of male relatives and lovers, these sisters, cousins, and wives frequently come back from the grave as vampires—in search of at least one last familial reunion. The evocation of dead women as saving ideals in Poe's poetry is sharply subverted in his short-story adaptations of the dead-woman-lover theme. Only once, in his late prose narrative "Eleonora," did Poe represent the death of a beautiful woman as an essentially uncomplicated event devoid of gender antagonism, feminine revenge, or male antipathy toward women. In his other love stories, men and woman may not be ultimately separated by the barrier of the grave, but their emotional estrangement and physical aggression perhaps pose an even greater chasm.

The compulsive male lovers found in Poe's short stories always appear, like his poetic melancholiacs, criminals, and murderers, to embody a full range of sadomasochistic motivations. They receive a particular admixture of terror and excitement from both the situation they have helped to create (the torturing of women that culminates in apparent death and premature burial) and the consequent psychological enslavement that follows (these women haunt the lives of their men long after death and into resurrection). But unlike the criminals and murderers in "The Tell-Tale Heart," "The Cask of Amontillado," or "The Black Cat," Poe's love stories feature emasculated males who wait and watch for the return of women they once tortured in one way or another. In contrast to this masculine passivity, the vampiric heroines of Poe's fiction return from the grave as active agents who inspire fear and revulsion in their conscience-stricken men. Poe may have insisted that the "death of a beautiful woman is, unquestionably, the most poetical topic in the world" (1379), but the beautiful women who populate his love stories are ultimately neither very poetical nor very dead. And while the male narrators in his poems remain locked in a singular state of permanent adoration toward the women who have abandoned them, in the short stories the masculine response is far more problematic and ambivalent.

"MORELLA" (1835)

First published in *The Southern Literary Messenger*, the tale involves the obsessive theme of psychic survival and return in bringing a woman back from the dead. The central theme of passionate longing for immortality—especially in a woman who is less flesh and blood than etherealized being—links "Morella" to its sister stories "Ligeia," "Berenice," and "The Fall of the House of Usher."

SETTING AND PLOT

One of the shortest of Poe's love plots, "Morella" revolves around the theme of a marriage that collapses because the male narrator loses interest in his wife. The setting for the story is not provided, and it is totally unimportant, since Poe supplies us with neither a historical context nor a specific geographical locale. In some of Poe's tales, setting is absolutely imperative to the narrative's meaning. The house and surrounding vegetation in "The Fall of the House of Usher," for example, are directly relevant to the events that occur as the plot unfolds. In other Poe tales, the emphasis is solely upon the internal landscape of a relationship or the protagonist's psyche (as in "The Tell-Tale Heart"). In "Morella," it is the domestic world of the narrator, his wife, and later, their daughter that remains the central theme of the tale. Setting and atmosphere are superfluous to the interdynamics of the family.

From the first paragraph of the tale, it is obvious that these two people should never have entered into matrimony: "[F]ate bound us together at the altar; and I never spoke of passion, nor thought of love" (234). Nevertheless, at first the couple establishes a certain degree of harmony in their relationship largely as a result of the intellectual capacities of Morella: "[H]er powers of mind were gigantic. I felt this, and, in many matters, became her pupil" (234). The narrator's fascination with his wife's erudition, however, does not blossom into a deeper appreciation of her as a human being, much less as a wife. In fact, very soon "the time had arrived when the mystery of my wife's manner oppressed me as a spell" (235).

The narrator's obvious unhappiness in his marriage eventually diminishes Morella's will to live, and she dies brokenhearted. It is interesting to note that the process of her physical and spiritual debilitation only begins after the narrator reaches the point where he yearns for "her gentle life decline—like shadows in the dying of the day" (236). But before the narrator gains the freedom he so desperately desires, his dying spouse levels a curse upon him: "Her whom in life thou didst abhor, In death thou shalt adore . . . the hours of thy happiness are over" (236).

At the very moment of death, Morella produces life: a daughter who bears an uncanny resemblance to her mother in both body and mind. Every time the narrator encounters his child, his participation in helping to kill her mother by the withholding of his affections causes him to feel great anguish. Although the narrator professes to love his daughter, he is unable to separate her identity from the detested mother. At her baptism, he impulsively chooses the name Morella for his yet nameless child, whereupon the daughter suddenly convulses and dies as the mother's curse is born out. Upon interment of the dead child in the ancestral vault, the narrator finds no trace of the bones of his deceased wife. The story concludes abruptly with this event, as the two Morellas have taken their revenge upon the bereft husband and father.

CHARACTERS

The first-person male narrator of "Morella" has much in common with the other male lovers and husbands in the tales that constitute Poe's love stories. All of them enter into far from healthy relationships with women that stretch the very limits of their endurance and sanity. While this man appreciates his wife's intellect, his tolerance for her eventually turns into an impatient desire to be free of their union and her very existence. Since his antipathy toward Morella mortally wounds her spirit, he is left saddled with a burden even greater than the marriage itself. In his daughter, he not only sees his former wife but is likewise constantly reminded by her presence of his own guilt as well as the curse

Morella bestowed upon him prior to dying: "[T]hat her eyes were like Morella's I could endure; but then they too often looked down into the depths of my soul with Morella's own intense and bewildering meaning. . . . I found food for consuming thought and horror—and for a worm that *would* not die" (238).

Morella and her daughter should be considered together as they function inseparably within the plot's unfolding. The daughter is an extension of her mother's revenge against the narrator at the same time she is a constant visible stimulus for his self-punishment. Morella herself is sister to many of Poe's other female protagonists in this group of love stories: treated badly by men who do not know how to express their love responsibly, the legacy of these women is not one of poetic inspiration or love's constancy. It appears, instead, in the form of a deathless curse from beyond the grave that strikes the respective male at the very center of his being.

THEMES

The dead Morella's reanimation through the body of her daughter should be read as the theme of a wife gaining final revenge over a husband for her feelings of unrequited love and the erosion of their marriage. The willingness to sacrifice her daughter in addition to her own urge toward self-annihilation suggests the level to which the narrator's passive aggression, emotional disaffection, and failure to love have distorted Morella's purposefulness as wife and mother. Similar to many of Poe's first-person male narrators, the husband in "Morella" is doomed by his own perverse desire for self-destruction (he is compelled to whisper Morella's name at the moment of his daughter's baptism) as much as he is victimized by a supernatural agency generated by his vengeful wife. Indeed, these two forces seem to work in a mysterious and inexorable collusion with one another.

"BERENICE" (1835)

This story was first published in the *Southern Literary Messenger* for March 1835. The tale is most appropriately linked to two other Poe love stories— "Morella" and "Ligeia"—and together the three narratives constitute what Poe scholars often refer to as the "marriage group."

SETTING AND PLOT

Similar to "Ligeia" and "The Oval Portrait," the setting for this story is a chamber; in "Berenice," it is a room filled with books rather than the arabesque tapestries or lifelike paintings that decorate the other two tales. Much of the first half of "Berenice" is a discussion of the narrator's boyhood and early adult-hood—a period spent "addicted body and soul to the most intense and painful medication" (226), with too much time spent alone in reverie and romantic lit-erature. From these earliest descriptions, it is clear that the narrator suffers, like many of Poe's men, from a chronic difficulty in distinguishing the realm of the fantastic from reality.

Berenice is introduced as the narrator's cousin, "[We] grew up together in my paternal halls. . . . I ill of health and buried in gloom—she agile, graceful, and overflowing with energy" (226). Although she was a beautiful woman, the narrator, like the husband in "Morella," claims to have never loved Berenice. Yet, "in an evil moment, I spoke to her of marriage" (229). Before the two are wed, however, Berenice weakens and becomes emaciated, perhaps the result of "a species of epilepsy not infrequently terminating in *trance* itself—trance very nearly resembling positive dissolution" (227). As the disease debilitates Berenice, particularly in the atrophy of her flesh, the narrator confesses that he has became more conscious of her teeth. This awareness turns quickly into an obsession, making it difficult for the man to concentrate upon anything else: "In the multiplied objects of the external world I had no thoughts but for the teeth. For these I longed with a phrenzied desire" (231). Eventually, the attrac-tion becomes so powerful that separating the teeth from Berenice's diseased body "could alone ever restore me to peace, in giving me back to reason" (231).

At midnight one evening, after being informed by a servant maiden that Berenice has died and been placed in a grave, the narrator sits alone in his li-brary "awakened from a confused and exciting dream" (232). Another servant then enters the library distraught with news of Berenice's violated grave, of the "piercing shriek of a female voice" that has disturbed the silence of the night, and of "a disfigured body enshrouded, yet still breathing, still palpitating, *still alive!*" (232). Although the narrative is a little ambiguous about all these post-mortem events, it appears that Berenice has been entombed prematurely and is not really dead but only in an epileptic coma. The servant then points to the narrator's clothes, "muddy and clotted with gore"; to his hand, "indented with the impress of human nails"; and, finally, to a shovel leaning against the wall (232–33). In horror, the narrator opens a box sitting upon a table to reveal ghastly dental instruments and thirty-two teeth that once belonged to Berenice.

CHARACTERS

Among his virtual asylum of fictional psychopaths, Poe's first-person narra-tor, whose baptismal name is Egaeus, in "Berenice" is one of his most disturbed individuals. His erratic behavior and obsessive dental fixation defy rational analysis or explanation. Egaeus is another of Poe's lost boys: his mother died when he was young, and perhaps, like Poe himself, he turned to books and the realm of his own imagination for relief from his interminable loneliness. Although he never convinces the reader that he is wholly normal or even sane, whatever connection Egaeus maintains with reality is gradually eroded as his cousin's physical health degenerates. Like many of the male narrators in these love stories, Egaeus maintains a love-hate relationship with the central female in his life. And although he claims that he "never loved her," he also acknowledges that "in an evil moment, I spoke to her of marriage" (229). Perhaps Egaeus remains, as he would have us believe, unconscious of his forced extraction of Berenice's teeth, but certainly the narrator is fully aware of his obsession and his desire for them. This compulsion is apparently so overwhelming that even Berenice's struggles and screams cannot dissuade him from completing the surgical procedure.

The narrator, like the husband in "Ligeia," is obsessed with a uniquely beautiful woman whose beauty is only enhanced because she is dying. But unlike the "Ligeia" narrator who claims to adore the entire influence of his wife, physical and spiritual, the maniacal protagonist of "Berenice" is highly selective in terms of what he chooses to emphasize and remember about his betrothed. As Berenice becomes more and more emaciated, especially as her lips pull back from her teeth and her head becomes more skull-like, the teeth reveal themselves and are transformed into the metaphor of his desire.

Berenice herself is hardly a character in this narrative at all; she is, in fact, more a dental specimen than human female. Her status is vague all through the tale, as the narrator remains wholly self-absorbed. Defined early on as a woman who "roamed carelessly through life with no thought of the shadows" (226), by midpoint of the story she is reduced merely to a set of molars and incisors, "long, narrow, and excessively white" (230).

THEMES

Egaeus's treatment of women in "Berenice" stands out as one of Poe's most shocking and repulsive depictions of woman-hating behavior. His violence against Berenice's oral orifice constitutes a violation that is on the level of rape, especially in light of her verbal protestations and physical struggle. The theme of the story is reduced to the psychological dynamics of the relationship itself. As is often the case in Poe, the real action of the narrative plot is internal, rather than external. The only physical action that occurs comes late in the tale, in the removal of Berenice's teeth. And the reader learns of this event secondhand, and as an occurrence that has already taken place. What Poe is most interested in exploring in so many of these tales—"Berenice" included—is the human attraction to the grotesque. Egaeus appears to follow Poe's aesthetic precept that beauty is enhanced when it is combined with an element of the bizarre and freakish. Indeed, the reader shares some of Egaeus's fascination, for this story hinges upon a developing emphasis upon the bizarre and the grotesque. As the narrator's behavior becomes more fixated upon the debilitated Berenice, we await his reaction with a certain increasing admixture of horror and excitement. To a very real extent, we find ourselves almost aligned with the narrator's twisted aesthetic and his desire to transcend the boundaries of decency.

As with many of Poe's male protagonists, it is clear that the narrator's erotic fascination with his cousin increases in proportion to the debilitating influence of epilepsy upon her body. The reader of "Berenice" is told that the narrator's response to her worsening illness is "a consuming curiosity" that leaves him "breathless and motionless" with "burning glances . . . riveted upon her person" (230). In many of Poe's tales, death for the female is eroticized by the male, suggesting at least an unconscious link between sexuality and sadistic desire.

His corresponding fascination with her teeth, however, is not so neatly explained. A psychoanalytic interpretation (see the Alternate Reading section at the end of chapter 6) might view the narrator's obsession and assault as a vaginal violation and destruction of the feminine (mother) in the narrator's symbolic mutilation of the entrance to the womb (mouth). The narrator's fixation on Berenice's teeth is an example of object fetishism: the narrator has unconsciously projected a generalized fear and aversion toward the female gender onto Berenice's teeth. In other words, if he can somehow manage to possess the teeth, he will symbolically destroy (or, in this particular case, defang) the threat that women represent to him. A psychiatrist might speak of this bizarre oral compulsion as an urge to control what the narrator fears most in females by first identifying—and then eliminating—the sites of their power. In her study of horror art and its relationship to the human body, feminist critic Barbara Creed defines the feminine mouth as a central location for expressing terror and the grotesque: "The body's boundaries are violated by the open bleeding mouth. Parallels with woman's other mouth and lips, which also bleed and also link with the outside, are obvious and are frequently underlined in the horror film. . . . For the mouth of the woman is used more and more as a displaced vagina—the opening through which woman is raped and inseminated by alien creatures" (152). The teeth-mouth-vagina connection, therefore, is of great importance to interpreting this Poe story, as the narrator's aversion toward women can be seen centered symbolically upon Berenice's teeth and his desire to possess them, thereby simultaneously rendering her helpless while alleviating his own sexual anxiety.

The concluding paragraphs of the text are as much a realization as they are a confession of the atrocity that the narrator is slowly beginning to comprehend. To commit this act, he has apparently willed himself into some level of dreamlike unconsciousness; on the other hand, the reader has been prepared for the grotesque extraction itself by the intensity and obsessional focus of the narrator on the teeth all through Berenice's illness. The oral surgery required a thirty-two-step operation, featuring a victim that was never anaesthetized. Only a man truly dedicated to his work—and sufficiently insensitive toward his victim—could perform such a gruesome activity in a sustained state of suspended consciousness. The oral extraction might also be read as a lover's violence unconsciously motivated against a woman whom he believes has abandoned him; her teeth, then, become a kind of grisly keepsake that, unlike mutable flesh, can be kept (safely in a box) forever.

"LIGEIA" (1838)

The first printing of this story, in the Baltimore *American Museum*, did not include the poem "The Conqueror Worm" which would appear for the first time when the story was reprinted in 1845. One of Poe's most famous love stories, and designated by him as a favorite, "Ligeia" features three prototypical Poe themes: the death of a mysterious and beautiful woman, the psychological instability of a bereaved narrator, and a cadaverous resurrection.

SETTING AND PLOT

For nearly the first half dozen pages that initiate this tale, a husband describes in detail his beautiful wife, Ligeia, who is now dead. We learn of her outstanding beauty: "The features of Ligeia were not of classic regularity—although I perceived that her loveliness was indeed 'exquisite' " (263). Likewise, we are informed of her vast intelligence: "[T]he learning of Ligeia was immense—such as I have never known in woman" (266). The core of Ligeia's philosophy, which is purportedly adapted from the mystic theologian Joseph Glavill, holds that the will is stronger than death or decay. If the passionate will for life is sufficiently vigorous, then the mind, soul, and body itself can conquer the ravages of time and disease. In addition to her beauty and her intelligence, however, there is a certain exotic air of mystery surrounding the darkly exotic Ligeia that captivates the narrator. She carries a nearly ethereal quality that makes her less flesh and blood than spirit. And as she grows ever closer to death, her "emaciated" demeanor is underscored by "the incomprehensible lightness and elasticity of her footfall. She came and departed as a shadow" (263).

It is certainly obvious to the reader that the narrator still grieves deeply for his lost wife. In spite of his pain—or perhaps because of it—he marries Lady Rowena Trevanion, who is the exact opposite, both physically and spiritually, to his first wife. The narrator is never very kindly disposed toward Rowena. He forces her to live in a dark and dreary apartment, separated from her family and friends. Their bridal chamber is similar to the interior of a haunted house, replete with terrifying images painted upon curtains induced to move through the assistance of specially designed artificial currents of air that make the images appear to become animated. Such deliberate efforts to unnerve his young wife show that the narrator did not marry Rowena for love: "That my wife dreaded the fierce moodiness of my temper—that she shunned me and loved me but little—I could not help perceiving; but it gave me rather pleasure than otherwise. I loathed her with a hatred" (272). Neither Poe nor the narrator ever make it clear why he marries her in the first place. But his level of distraction and urge to torment Rowena help the reader to suspect that Rowena's untimely death is more connected to the narrator than he would have us believe. According to his explanation, one night "three or four drops of a brilliant and ruby colored fluid" (273) were mysteriously deposited in a glass of Rowena's wine. After drinking the contaminated libation (the narrator conveniently refrained from warning her about the mysterious fluid), she lapsed into a coma and died. Although he keeps a nocturnal vigil over Rowena's corpse, the narrator's grief is never for her; his thoughts continue to center upon Ligeia. At the conclusion of the tale, Rowena's body is inexplicably reanimated, lurches off the bed, and reveals itself to be Ligeia. The narrator greets this phenomenon with a mixture of "unutterable horror and awe" (275).

CHARACTERS

Since everything that occurs in this tale is filtered through a first-person narrator, the reader is left in the uncomfortable position of trying to figure out how much of what this narrator reveals is truthful. In fact, we know very little about the narrator's personality. This is, in part, because so much of the plot revolves around his description of Ligeia herself; the narrator's role, for at least the first third of the story, is to serve as Ligeia's mirror—defining her physical beauty and mental acuity.

The speaker's credibility is weakened by at least two facts that are certain: his mind is obsessed with the dead Ligeia and he is addicted to opium. As a result, the narrator's perception of reality is radically distorted; indeed, one might argue that he no longer possesses the ability to distinguish objective reality from self-constructed fantasy: "Wild visions, opium-engendered, flitted, shadow-like, before me" (274). If we take this character at his word, this becomes a story about the triumph of the human spirit over death: Ligeia wills herself back to life by vamping Rowena's body. If we discredit the narrator's version, then everything in the narrative falls under question, since its unreal events merely illustrate the excesses of a hyperstimulated imagination. No other horror tale by Poe combines such simplicity of plot with such equivocal complexity of meaning and motivation.

Typical to other fated ladies in Poe's fiction, Ligeia, whose odd name is both poetically exotic and, in its pronunciation (Lie-gee-ah) draws emphasis to her haunting dark eyes, is an admixture of beauty and disease, an object of desire and fear. She maintains a remarkable power over her husband's imagination—in death as well as in life. With her long black hair, pale face, dark eyes, long eyelashes, and statuesque figure, Ligeia exemplifies the romantic ideal of the nineteenth century. Her long black hair and piercing dark eyes link her effectively to the nineteenth century's stereotype of the romantic woman: exotic, erotic, mysterious, less tied to the mundane than to the supernal.

It is interesting to note that nineteenth-century readers would have recognized in the brunette Ligeia the same feminine archetype that the twentieth century has bestowed upon the beautiful blonde. She is, however, also strong willed and highly intelligent, which would make her an exception to the popular ideal of early nineteenth-century womanhood. In this way, she anticipates (and was an actual inspiration for) the aesthetic ideal of the femme fatale found in the Pre-Raphaelites and which, through them, was to pass into French Symbolist and Decadent art movements at the end of the century. Their work featured women whose radiant beauty was aligned with an imperial detachment and an air of power and domination. Men worship the femme fatale out of fear as much as adoration; they aspire to be the powerless victim of the furious rage of a beautiful woman. Their love is a martyrdom, their pleasure pain. In accordance with this conception of the fatal woman, the male lover usually maintains a passive attitude, as in Poe's "Ligeia"; he is obscure, and inferior in both physical status and mental capacities to the woman, who stands in the same relation to him as the female spider or praying mantis to their respective males. The character of Susan Stone Morelli (Nicole Kidman) in the film *To Die For* is a contemporary version of the femme fatale, whose prototype dates back to Ligeia and her dark sisters who emerged later in the nineteenth century.

Ligeia's role in Poe's tale, however, is rather restricted: similar to other Poe women, she is more an object of adoration than an active participant in the shaping of events. Although Ligeia dies midway through the tale, her presence is keenly felt through the narrator's obsessive recollections, and by the end of the narrative she once again occupies center stage.

Lady Rowena Trevanion of Tremaine is blonde, blue-eyed, and perhaps the most victimized character in Poe's entire canon. If Ligeia embodies the exotic and supernal nature of romantic femininity, Rowena is a figure from the normal, mundane world that views excursions into the bizarre or supernatural as purely morbid. Perhaps the narrator marries her to help him forget the Lady Ligeia, but from the honeymoon on the contrast she offers only makes him long even more for his dark-haired soulmate. Although her role in the tale is too restricted for readers to align themselves closely with her fate, the treatment she receives nonetheless inspires a certain disgust toward the narrator who remains so callous in his attitude and machinations. Readers also recognize that she is dangerously acquiescent and receptive—unfortunately in the wrong place, at the wrong time, and with the wrong man. Betrayed by her family, who allow her to marry such an unsuitable husband, Rowena is then tormented by the latter, who is at least indirectly implicated in her illness and death. Even her own corpse is stolen from Rowena, as it is used by Ligeia to complete "this hideous drama of revivification" (276). In this special variety of vampire tale, Lady Rowena is the sleeping beauty whose soul and body, rather than her blood, are necessary for Ligeia's return.

THEMES

The narrator of "Ligeia" is at best a confused individual. He goes from a state of near childlike dependency on his first wife to aversion and hatred toward his second. At first glance, it would seem that this man possesses dualistic attitudes toward women and marriage. But as critic J. Gerald Kennedy reminds us, the narrator "never suspects the connection between his adoration of Ligeia and his contempt for Rowena . . . that the plot carried out in the Gothic chamber is ultimately a plot against Woman" (126). The cruelty that the narrator so readily and shamelessly projects on the innocent Rowena indicates that his attitude toward women borders on the pathological. We should not be distracted by his professed love for Ligeia; even this relationship is marked by certain unconscious elements of resentment: first, that Ligeia is the narrator's acknowledged superior and, second, that she dares abandon him to languish in his present state of isolation and discontent. To mollify this condition, the narrator goes out in search of another wife, virtually purchases her from her family, and then proceeds to take out on Rowena all the unresolved feelings of hostility he still harbors toward Ligeia. Rowena is never known, either by the reader or her tormentor, as an individual woman. She is, instead, merely woman, a surrogate lover-wife who becomes victim of her husband's desire for revenge against women in general—and Ligeia specifically.

The narrator of "Ligeia" loses his wife before his passion sobers and sours, which is the fate that befalls the husband in "Morella": "The time had now arrived when the mystery of my wife's manner oppressed me as a spell" (235). But it is likewise clear from his behavior toward Rowena that Ligeia's mate harbors a similar antagonism toward women that links him closely to the narrator in "Morella." And given more time in their marriage, it is possible that he would have committed ever more overt acts of cruelty toward Ligeia herself.

The supernatural resurrection that concludes "Ligeia" is another thematic element that this tale shares with Poe's other love stories. Assuming that the speaker has not hallucinated its very occurrence, the reanimated corpse that stumbles off the deathbed is a synthesis of Rowena-Ligeia. Thus, it is no wonder that the "vamped" creature "Shrinks from [the] touch" of the narrator, even as he manages to overcome his own terror sufficiently to move toward it (277). Rowena-Ligeia can only free itself from the "ghastly cerements which had confined it" (277) by avoiding the man who, at least in part, is responsible for orchestrating this macabre situation in the first place. The story's theme of a man's longing for his dead wife merges with his urge to bring her back, even at the possible expense of another woman's life and his own sanity. Caught between desire and denial, the narrator's own reaction to the tale's climactic supernatural event is decidedly mixed: he is terrified by the reanimation at the same time as he has been desperately hoping for it to occur. The narrator may have won his wish to be reunited with Ligeia, but the ending of this tale comes with many unresolved ambivalences that would seem to preclude a happy ending for either the speaker or his revivified wives.

"THE FALL OF THE HOUSE OF USHER" (1839)

One of the most famous and frequently anthologized of all Edgar Allan Poe's fictional works, it has probably drawn the most scholarly attention of any Poe narrative. The tale was first published in the September 1839 volume of *Burton's Gentleman's Magazine*.

SETTING AND PLOT

On a "dull, dark, and soundless day in the autumn of the year" (317), the nameless narrator approaches the mansion of his boyhood friend, Roderick Usher. The Usher house itself is a very important element in the story. It stands astride a mountain lake and appears particularly foreboding by the vacant stare of its windows and a crack or fissure that runs up the center of the façade. Inside this Gothic dwelling the narrator encounters the Usher twins, Roderick and Madeline, whose complexions are cadaverous and who both suffer from "excessive nervous agitation" (321–22). Roderick's condition is worsened by the fact that his sister appears to be dying slowly of an unknown disease.

The narrator attempts to bring some measure of relief to this intensely depressive household. But soon he and the reader come to realize that the Usher melancholia simply runs too deep. Madeline and Roderick are the last of the Usher legacy. They feel cursed by the guilt of some secret sin, perhaps related to a singular and vaguely incestual bond that Roderick may share with his sister, and both siblings appear resigned to their mutual doom. One night Roderick informs the narrator that Madeline has died. Although the narrator notices a "faint blush upon the bosom and face, and that suspiciously lingering smile upon the lip" (329), the narrator helps Roderick inter her in a vault located in the basement of the house. In the days that follow, Roderick appears even more distracted and disconnected; he loses all interest in his artistic endeavors and spends his waking hours wandering through the mansion aimlessly. On a particularly stormy night, the narrator tries to alleviate Roderick's condition by reading to him. The story is interrupted by Madeline's sudden appearance, as Roderick announces, "*We have put her living in the tomb!*" (334). The rest of the tale is a whirlwind of events as the narrator witnesses the primal horror of Madeline's walking cadaver, "trembling and reeling to and fro on the threshold," collapsing finally into the room to embrace her brother and bear "him to the floor a corpse, and a victim to the terrors he had anticipated" (335). As if cued in this final moment, or maybe even compelling it to occur, the house itself begins to crumble and collapses down upon the pair. Unable to account rationally for the reappearance of Lady Madeline and the corresponding destruction of the house, the narrator is forced to flee the wreckage before he, too, is consumed by the final fall of this fallen world.

CHARACTERS

There are three human characters in this story, but there is also an inhuman force that shapes events as much or more than the humans involved: the Usher mansion itself. A defining presence in this text, the Usher mansion is a direct architectural descendant from the eighteenth-century Gothic novel, especially Horace Walpole's *Castle of Otranto* and Anne Radcliffe's *The Mysteries of Udolpho*. The Usher house—the first truly *American* haunted house—has inspired generations of horror homes that followed: from Shirley Jackson's superanimated Hill House, to the Bates mansion in the film *Psycho*, to Stephen King's Marsten House in *Salem's Lot* and the Overlook Hotel in *The Shining*. There is an unexplained evil energy that permeates all these physical dwellings. This force originates in Poe's tale as a malign will that not only restricts the inhabitants that dwell within to the confines of the house itself but also pursues their loss of sanity and sense of inevitable doom. The Usher mansion is alive with an infernal power unto itself; it and the surrounding bog exude an evil atmosphere. Some interpreters of this story have even suggested that the house functions as a vampire in this tale, preying upon its human inhabitants by gradually draining them of their psychic energies.

Roderick Usher is in many ways the archetypal Poe protagonist. Cut off from all external reality and menaced by the mansion that is his home, Usher, the dying artist, anticipates his own destruction and does nothing to prevent it. In fact, one might argue that, like so many of Poe's heroes, Roderick revels in his pain, and that is why he summons the narrator in the first place: to exhibit his anguish to someone else and thereby deepen his own awareness of it. Morbidly sensitive to a world beyond the apprehension of mere mortals, Usher is much more complex than either he or the narrator is willing to reveal. For example, if he possesses such acute powers of intuition and sensitivity, why doesn't he appreciate the danger he and his sister are in and follow the narrator out into freedom? In other words, what ultimately plagues Usher and causes him to accept his destruction so meekly? Of course, Poe never fully explains this, but readers are left to ponder about the "secret sin" that Roderick shares with his sister. Perhaps the onus of guilt associated with that sin erodes both their spirits, making death and madness welcome releases from the daily reminders of their shared burden. In the end, his final madness is precipitated by his guilt over the premature burial of his sister Madeline, and equally as significant, his refusal to aid in releasing her, despite his knowledge of her struggles within the coffin.

If Roderick Usher's personality remains a perplexing mystery in this tale, then twin sister Madeline's is even more so. Seen only twice in the entire story, and the second time as a revenging revenant, Madeline Usher is less flesh and blood woman than blonde smoke, moving like a silent wraith through the rooms of the mansion. Her haunting presence never fails to disturb Usher and the narrator, even before either man believes that she has been buried prematurely. Only at the end of the narrative, when she embraces her brother and initiates the self-implosion of the mansion, do we see Lady Madeline as an entity capable of action. But even then, the reader is forced to wonder how and why she returns from the crypt. She appears to possess barely enough strength to rise from her deathbed, much less escape the confinement of the basement burial vault, climb the stairs to the top floor of the mansion, and collapse upon her brother.

The narrator of this tale is one of the few apparently reliable first-person storytellers found in Poe's tales of terror and suspense, and the only "normal" male voice in the writer's entire collection of love stories. Poe separates the narrator in this story from his central protagonist—one embodies rational convention, the other obsession and desire—in much the same way as the writer introduces a secondary narrator to describe the events in the detective stories (see chapter 6). Unrelated to the Ushers except by way of a boyhood friendship with Roderick, the narrator has very little in common with his host. (Usher's artistic endeavors only baffle the narrator even as he appreciates their strangeness.) The narrator's purpose in this tale appears to be that of a rationalist recording a series of bizarre and supernatural events; his explanation of these events throws Usher's wildly erratic temperament into high relief. Since the narrator is always the controlling consciousness of the story, the reader enters the weird world of the Usher siblings with him and leaves it at the end. On the other hand, there is some evidence to suggest that the narrator of this tale is not completely above reproach. His involvement in the entombment of Madeline, trusting Roderick's unstable judgment without first proving to himself that she is indeed dead, perhaps indicates that he may have more in common with brother Roderick than he would like his audience to realize.

THEMES

The theme of "The Fall of the House of Usher" is the helplessness of humanity in the face of powers that are both larger than the individual human and committed to his obliteration. This theme is a quintessential element of the horror tale, that human beings are destined to struggle against forces of evil that are too great to be overcome. Sometimes these powers can be endured, but in Usher's case they prove totally overwhelming. The tale has been the object of diverse critical interpretations, perhaps more so than any other Poe work, ranging from explanations that explore the curse that is causing the mansion's steady decay, to the role of Roderick Usher as an artist figure, to discussions on the transference of psychic energy that is passed among brother, sister, and the parasitic house. More than any other Poe tale, the question of who is the vampire in this story remains completely open ended. Some critics have maintained that Madeline has been slowly vamping her brother all along, and that their physical embrace at the tale's climax signals the final, consummate rendering of her vampiric feeding. Neither ever wholly dead nor alive, Madeline inhabits the nether state of the restless vampire spirit. Her pursuit and collapse upon Roderick parallels the body positioning of the vampire draining its victim in a sexual embrace. But the possibility of Roderick as a sinister manipulator of his sister in her death and premature interment, even the house itself as the source that controls the ultimate destiny of the Usher twins, is just as plausible.

Because of Usher's loneliness, alienation, his immersion in art, his secret guilt, and his apparent damnation by forces beyond his control, some readers of this tale have found parallels between Roderick and Poe himself. Both men are tortured by acute internal ailments. Usher's hair, bushy eyebrows and dark brooding eyes resemble those of Poe himself. Usher's unholy bond with Madeline has also prompted some critics to recall Poe's own maternal and sexual confusions (e.g., his quasi-incestual bond with his second cousin, Virginia) that involved him fatally in the search for an ideal woman to bring him ultimate solace from his life's various torments.

At the core of this story is the presence of an enormous, unfathomable evil, even if it remains uncertain whether that evil is generated by Roderick,

Madeline, their familial bond, or something inherited from the past that is greater than both of them. In any event, this evil remains too great to be challenged, much less overcome; it can only be experienced. And, of course, the experience proves overwhelming for everyone: the Ushers, the narrator, perhaps even the reader. Whether the reader chooses to interpret the story as an autobiographical reflection of Poe himself, as a tale of mutual vampirism and annihilation centering upon a fusion of the halves of male-female archetypes, or even as a prototype for the haunted house tale, "Usher" inspires a response of fascination mixed with disquietude that was always Poe's goal in the achievement of his horror art.

"THE OVAL PORTRAIT" (1842)

First published in *Graham's Magazine* under the title "Life in Death," the tale was revised, retitled, and printed under the name "The Oval Portrait" in the *Broadway Journal* of April 1845. While this story is frequently anthologized, over the years it has received very little scholarly attention.

SETTING AND PLOT

The tale takes place in a gloomy chateau among the Apennines (a range of mountains traversing the length of Italy), where a wounded soldier, a victim of some unnamed war taking place at some unknown time, who is also the work's first-person narrator, seeks refuge. In the process of his convalescence, the narrator is much taken by the paintings that adorn the walls, especially an oval portrait of "a young girl just ripening into womanhood" (482). As he contemplates the painting ever more deeply, he comes to appreciate that the portrait's entrancing effect is to be found in its "absolute *life-likeliness* of expression" (482). Drawn to the composition, the narrator consults a book at his bedside that describes the paintings and their histories. He learns that the woman who sat for the oval portrait was very much in love with the artist, who was also her husband. His truest love, however, was reserved for his art. As she posed for his work, he "took a fervid and burning pleasure in his task, and wrought day and night to depict her who so loved him, yet who grew daily more dispirited and weak" (483). Upon completing the masterpiece after many months of labor on it, he discovers that this model-wife has expired. Perhaps most horrifying about the conclusion, it is never clear just how long the woman has been dead before the artist realizes this fact.

CHARACTERS

The wounded soldier-narrator of this story resembles closely the narrator of "The Fall of the House of Usher": both men are drawn into intense male-female relationships that mystify at the same time that they horrify. Although essentially removed from the central action of both plots, these narrators cannot help but find themselves strongly influenced by what they learn and witness. In "The Oval Portrait," this shaping process is so affective that the narrator "bade Pedro to close the heavy shutters of the room" (481), literally following the fated couple into the same cloistered chamber where the murder-artistic production occurred. On at least one level, the narrator becomes as much a captive to the painting as the model and painter were to its creation. He becomes so fascinated with the painting and the history of its origins that he shows little interest in anything else. By the end of the story, he has "disappeared" into the narrative describing the painting composition, himself becoming part of its history.

The artist in this tale is another of Poe's alternate vampire figures, working day and night to drain the life force of his subject and transfer it to a pallid canvas. The lifelikeness of the model's vital colors reveals a portrait literally painted in blood. The artist is passionate but austere, perhaps most similar to Roderick Usher, in that the self-absorption of both men renders them incapable of rescuing the women in their lives until it is too late. The artist is definitely very talented, but he is also unwilling to recognize or appreciate what is most important in his life. Poe makes this point emphatically when he informs us that the pride and will of the painter is so great that he "*would* not see that the light which fell so ghastly in that lone turret withered the health and spirits of his bride" (483). His artistic legacy means more to him than the woman he loves; she becomes merely a means to this end.

The model in this tale is not only beautiful; she is also vital. This admixture makes her victimization all the more poignant, and the reader can appreciate why the soldier-narrator is so moved by the painting's history. She is another of Poe's passively silent beauties, a "humble and obedient" (483) woman who willingly puts up with her husband's strenuous demands out of a pathetic effort to please him and to remain at the center of his attention. Her tragic self-sacrifice is a consequence of her meekness as much as it is the result of the artist's insensitivity. The model is reduced to an obsessional object whose very humanity is the price for artistic immortality.

THEMES

Poe's short tale of murder-artistic production is effectively rendered. In this portrait of a man obsessed with his art and a woman so in love with her man that she fears to challenge his obsession, we find a subtle critique on the themes of art and love. For Poe, the artist in this tale suffers from a selfish blindness in his willingness to sacrifice his love for a flesh-and-blood woman in exchange for creative immortality. His female model similarly suffers from a blindness born out of adoration, feminine passivity, and fear of possibly alienating or angering her imperious artist-husband. Her prolonged silence—even as her sense of doom becomes more inevitable, at least to her—is a subtle reminder that a pattern of sustained abuse is only possible when a victim agrees to cooperate in her own victimization.

Poe's portrait of the artist as vampire can be compared with Nathaniel Hawthorne's similarly destructive artist figure in "The Birthmark" and the murderous conditions related in Robert Browning's "My Last Duchess." The male artists in all of these narratives willingly sacrifice their subjects—wives they supposedly love—in the pursuit of artistic perfection. In each case, the female subjects ironically participate in their own destruction out of their devotion to their husband-artists. The model in the oval portrait, "yet smiled on and still on, uncomplainingly" (483) because she believed her husband's work (and his will) to be of more importance than her own happiness—and, ultimately, her own life.

ALTERNATE READING: FEMINISM

Feminist theory begins with the simple premise that prejudice against women has long been embedded in Western culture, social institutions, and general attitudes. At the same time, the goal of feminism is to challenge this situation so that both men and women will come to view females as valuable individuals possessing the same rights and privileges as every man. Historians argue for different origins of feminism, but certainly a major moment that marks its development dates back to the suffragist movements at the end of the nineteenth and early twentieth centuries. During this time, women fought for the right to vote but also became active in social issues of the day, particularly those that affected women directly: health care, child welfare, education, and government-sponsored family assistance. Modern feminism, however, began in the late 1960s and early 1970s, as women involved in national and international social movements to end the Vietnam war, confront racism, and change existing political structures turned their critical gaze toward examining gender constructions that separate males from females to keep the latter in subservient positions. These gendered norms and expectations are transmitted and encoded, feminists have argued, through all existing cultural information media: advertising, television, movies, songs, fashion, childbearing, and literature.

The feminist movement has influenced nearly every academic course of study in the humanities, social sciences, and even some of the sciences. Its influence has forced scholars in all these fields to expand traditional perceptions, and, in many cases, to reevaluate long-held assumptions, subjects and topics worthy of examination, and even the methodology used to conduct research.

In the literary field, feminist scholars challenged both the traditional canon, where they found the discipline dominated by male writers, and the vast body of interpretative criticism on these writers that reflected a similar male bias. They discovered that most women characters in male-generated fiction held either peripheral roles or were portrayed as beautiful goddesses, evil seducers, submissive wives, and shrews. Feminist critics questioned the contexts for these stereotypes: first, that they were constructed almost exclusively by male authors; and, second, that literary scholarship had so far failed to challenge these fictional stereotypes and the contrasting status of male characters occupying dominant and more diversified roles.

For feminist theorists, a whole new set of interpretations and priorities were necessary in order to redress the discrimination against women as both the subjects of texts (literary characters) and as ignored originators of texts (authors). As a consequence, in the past twenty-five years, the Western literary canon has expanded to include women writers, while feminist scholars have written a body of criticism that analyzes various aspects of gender dynamics reflected in both male- and female-authored texts. A fundamental position for feminist theory is that man is the subject of most texts, the one who defines meaning, while woman is the object—or other—having her existence defined by the male. This gender positioning reflects the biases of a patriarchal society, which assumes the superiority of the male over the female. Feminist critics want to demonstrate the errors in the logic of gender oppression, believing that women are human beings in their own right, not appendages of husbands and fathers nor the articulated sum of patriarchal opinions. To free themselves from such limitations, feminist literary scholars pursue critical positions that challenge whatever assumptions have helped to shape literary images of female inferiority and oppression. By reexamining the established literary canon, this time with a focus on the roles available for women, their relationships to males, and their respective positioning in a given text, feminist scholars have helped to revivify the art of literary criticism by providing a context that views women characters in light of male domination and social oppression.

Since a feminist critic often begins by examining the treatment of female characters and the roles they occupy within a narrative, Poe's love stories invite a feminist reading because women are of central importance to these tales. Yet, in spite of their importance (note how often the title of a Poe tale or poem is named after a female), his literary women are almost interchangeable. They come to share many traits in common: otherworldly beings in possession of extraordinary beauty, untimely and mysterious illnesses and deaths, and a strange (and strained) affiliation with men who are paradoxically obsessed and repulsed by them.

At first, Poe's women would appear to conform to stereotypes of the nineteenth-century romantic heroine; their collective silence reflective of their status as objects of distant loveliness and/or poetic inspiration. For despite their sickly beauty, it is important to note how seldom women characters in Poe—either in his poetry or his prose—get to think, possess an opinion, or say anything for themselves. Their language, on those rare occasions when they are permitted actual speech, is always filtered through the voice of the first-person male narrator. Masculine control over the feminine in these texts is mirrored in the very structure of the narrative itself. Essentially, Poe's females are the creations of the males in their lives—their reading habits, fashion sense, unflagging loyalty, and supernal beauty—known to readers only through biased descriptions generated, and manipulated, by male storytellers. All of these tales take place in complete isolation. Other than the narrator and the dead-wife-lover, there are few other characters/people present in these tales. No friends, no family, no nosy neighbors. And when there is an outsider present, as in "The Fall of the House of Usher," he is helpless to exert any influence over either the events that unfold or the characters with whom he interacts. Moreover, the settings for these stories are likewise suggestive of the bizarre and enforced isolation we find in their characterizations: houses on the edge of deserted and dreary pools of stagnant water, rooms filled with animated tapestries of horrific and unsettling figures. A feminist analysis would call particular attention to these facts, emphasizing that the erratic behavior of Poe's female protagonists can be fully understood only in light of their consistent subordination to men who have deliberately cut all ties to any stimulus from the external world.

Poet and translator Charles Baudelaire observed in 1856 that all of Poe's women are "strikingly delineated as though by an adorer," meaning that what the reader learns about any of them is shaped by the limited perception of the men who loved them. More than fifty years later, Marie Bonaparte, in her psychoanalytic biography of Poe, responded to Baudelaire's observation by complicating it even further. She not only recognized adoration in the descriptions of these first-person male narrators, but also, conversely, a genuine element of fear surrounding the objects (women) of their adoration. For Bonaparte, the Poe male is "An adorer . . . who dares not approach the object of his adoration, since he feels it surrounded by some fearful, dangerous mystery" (209–10). The reason the male in Poe's love stories "dares not approach the object of his adoration" is largely that he is responsible for having done something terrible to the object whom he adores; meanwhile, his woman has become a "fearful, dangerous mystery" because she has transformed herself from passive being into unearthly and highly unpoetical antagonist. Unlike the female inspirations that mark his poetry, the women in Poe's love stories cannot and did not stay dead; many metamorphose into female vampires who come back to life in aggressive search for the men they once loved. Nothing or no one is ever wholly settled or dead in Edgar Allan Poe's universe; in fact, the horror of his tales is often found in the hideous reanimation of forms—organic as well as inorganic—presumed to be dormant.

Novelist and critic D.H. Lawrence was the first to recognize that Poe's love stories were explicit vampire tales. Poe is not supplying vampires according to the tradition that Bram Stoker developed in the novel *Dracula*. For in place of undead creatures that require blood to continue their immortality, Poe's vampires feast upon the spirit or psyche, rather than the flesh, of those whom they once loved. Another issue that always appears to complicate Lawrence's observation is the question of who is vamping whom in these stories? While the women are frequently the apparent vampires at the end of these tales, the male characters are the ones who usually "vamp," or feed upon the women in the actual course of their relationship. In the course of most of these narratives, Poe's lovers exchange vampiric roles in order to consume one another in a psychological and intellectual sense (Twitchell, 125). Unlike the vampires of Hollywood films and Anne Rice novels, they demonstrate little real eroticism; rather, their "love" is transformed into a desire for domination. Poe's version of the vampire tale is less a vehicle for venting repressed eroticism and more a paradigm for expressing love that is too demanding and gender relationships that have grown too confining.

Acutely sensitive to the life-and-death struggle that is disguised as romantic love in Poe's tales of amorous relationships, Lawrence interpreted the return of Poe's post-burial females as the culminating event of a gendered conflict for control; or, in Lawrence's cryptic phrasing, a "knowledge of the other." "To try to *know* any living being is to try to suck the life out of that being. . . . men, beware, a thousand times more of the woman who wants to *know* you or *get* you, what you are. It is the temptation of a vampire fiend, is this knowledge" (67). While it is uncertain precisely what Lawrence meant by this "knowledge" that Poe's revenant women seek to steal from their men, it is clear, however, that they do return to exact some kind of punishment or revenge against the males. But where does this undercurrent of feminine rage come from? Here it is most helpful to keep in mind feminist theory as a means for explaining why these women behave as they do. Poe's programmatic elimination of women has come under increasing scrutiny in light of feminist criticism, and understandably so, for this pattern "raises troubling questions about an inherent misogyny" (Kennedy, 113). In addition to burying their female love-relatives prematurely ("Ligeia" and "The Fall of the House of Usher"), subjecting them to intense physical torture and manipulation ("Berenice," "The Oval Portrait," and "Ligeia"), and nurturing a deepening revulsion for a wife's intellectual and physical vitality ("Morella"), Poe's male narrators force these women to cohabit deliberately constructed worlds of decadent isolation, destructive artistic pursuits, and antisocial behavior that make it quite impossible for even the healthiest of women to remain sane, much less free of life-threatening disease. And once she succumbs to an illness that drains away her vitality, the male, who often harbors a not-so-subtle desire to kill his love object, is plunged immediately into guilt.

Ligeia, Rowena, Madeline Usher, Morella, the model in "The Oval Portrait," and Berenice inhabit virtually identical worlds: they are, to greater or lesser degrees, nineteenth-century obsessional objects under male control, exploited and abused women whose lives are either physically circumscribed or spiritually drained by the insensitive males who dominate them. In "Ligeia," "The Oval Portrait," and "Usher," these male fantasy realms are constructed under the rubric of obsessional love; in "Morella" and "Berenice," male antipathy for the feminine manifests itself undisguised in overt and grotesque levels of violence and disrespect. In both these instances, however, eccentric males demand an absolute possession of the feminine, even if this control finally results in the mutual destruction of both genders.

In the nineteenth century, women were considered little more than property to be owned by men; under patriarchal dominion economically and culturally, their status was just a level above that of a slave. Since all these Poe women live with men who are either blood relatives or husband-lovers, they have been socialized to accept whatever patriarchal design is imposed upon them—even to the point of forced dental extractions and murder. Unable to divorce themselves from unhealthy relationships with men who either no longer love them or demonstrate their affection in wholly unacceptable ways, these women have few options other than to endure their situations. Is it any wonder, then, that so many of these texts produce similar lady revenants whose final actions are motivated by what Marie Bonaparte has called "some fearful, dangerous mystery," and who emerge from their crypts seeking violent retribution against the men who are responsible for placing them there? As Poe scholar Joan Dayan posits: "In Poe's tales about women, marriage turns what was cherished into what is scorned" (202). In Poe's love stories the male's overbearing love destroys the female protagonist by violating her psychic—and, oftentimes, her physical—space. As he has vamped his woman's independence, she, in turn, following the paradigm for these tales, returns from the dead to consume him. Her transformation into a revenant should be seen as the upshot of an unholy tryst between the narrator's neurotic guilt and the compulsion of a pre-feminist spirit to rise up from passivity to revenge.

5

Tales of Psychological Terror, Homicide, and Revenge

If it were possible somehow to graph the material covered so far in this book, one distinguishing element that would plot a line from Poe's poetry, through his love stories, to this chapter—analyzing his narratives of homicide and revenge—is that the level of violence and psychological distortion would rise exponentially. Poe's poetry establishes static tableaus of beauty mixed with pain in the mind of the poetic narrator; he is, finally, as much an outsider to the narrative "action" as the dead woman whom he mourns. The vampiric love stories offer a similar plot design: the male protagonist passively awaits the destruction and return of the woman he simultaneously fears and adores. Poe's tales of homicide and revenge, on the other hand, feature aggressively proactive narrators who come ultimately to define themselves in the crimes they commit.

Poe's poetry, love stories, and tales of terror mixed with murder and suspense all feature compressed and circumscribed worlds populated by psyches out of control. One of the most unnerving qualities in Poe's fiction is its circumscription of mental space—that is, the construction of tales that feature the mind closing in on itself. His work centers upon interior crises where the human mind is under assault, and its primary nemesis is itself. A madman's version of reality, in Poe's view, was more deserving of attention than a more rational perception. It was not that Poe himself was a madman, an erroneous judgment that dates back to the nineteenth century but still continues to be made today by people who insist upon identifying Poe with his characters. As a writer, he simply felt that the world of the interior self—its dreams, nightmares, fears, and delusions—needed to be expressed artistically. Horror author H.P. Lovecraft recognized Poe's aptitude for transposing private torments into "a master's vision of the terror that stalks about within us. He penetrated to every festering horror in the gaily painted mockery called existence" (54). Since this interior state was more real for his particular protagonists than elements found in an objective exterior reality, Poe's first-person narrators force the reader to enter a world where psychosis and dementia reign. It is a world of gross distortion, unreal construction, and irrational propensities toward violent behavior.

These traits can be found in fictional characterizations throughout Poe's canon, but nowhere are they more outstanding than in his classic tales of homicide and revenge. And it is always interesting to note that, at least in popular culture, Poe is most famous for these tales of violence and terror. Perhaps this is so because the narratives are so well crafted—the language itself constructed in a way that enriches the suspense and horror of the event being described. Or maybe it is simply our attraction to violence, as Americans, and as human beings. Poe takes us into the interior world of human monsters who have overcome, at least to some extent, the social and moral taboo that condemns the act of murder. And we are fascinated by what this journey reveals—just as we long to know more about what motivated the teenage killers at Columbine High School or the serial murderer whose most recent work was profiled in yesterday's newspaper or cop show. Unlike the poems or the vampiric love stories, Poe's narratives of murders and murdering pivot around acts of violence and the comission of criminality; the interior darkness of these stories is not lightened by any degree of love or affection, however distorted or distracted. As we move from Poe's poetry to his love stories, to his tales of homicidal criminals, it is clear that while still inhabiting a highly subjective interior arena of delusion and confusion, we are also following protagonists who are moving generally from a realm of obsessive love to one of obsessive violence.

The paradigmatic Poe tale of murder and revenge displays several unifying traits. Like the poetry and love stories, the protagonists in "The Tell-Tale Heart," "The Imp of the Perverse," "The Black Cat," "The Cask of Amontillado," and "The Masque of the Red Death" all emerge from similar conditions. They spend too much time alone, divorced from meaningful social community, family, and friends. As their worlds become literally more circumscribed, their psychological conditions simultaneously narrow—leading to pathological distortion, obsessive behavior, delusions of grandeur, and a loss of psychic balance. As their psychological frames of reference narrow, their abilities to behave rationally, to make accurate judgments and healthy choices, are gradually eroded. As this occurs, thoughts of murder and the pursuit of selfish pleasures are inevitable consequences.

Unlike the essentially *passive* narrators found in the poetry and love tales, however, Poe's homicidal men are in *active* rebellion against some restrictive moral or physical law that has denied them access to an imaginary realm associated with freedom and self-expression. While the narrators in the poetry appear almost serene in the ethereal contemplation of loss and the death of the beautiful, the obsessions of Poe's sociopathic criminals usually center upon a person or object that symbolizes personal oppression: an intrusive wife, an intolerable insult, a black cat, a vulturelike eye. In other words, the homicidal mind, although anguished and tormenting, still wishes to inhabit the realm where the poet resides—and murder is the only drug or vehicle that will transport him there. In order to obtain this desired state of tranquility, all symbols of outside oppression and propriety must first be destroyed.

Immediately after concluding their gruesome work, Poe's homicidal narrators feel an initial sense of euphoria; they have liberated themselves psychologically at the same time that they have eliminated the source of their personal oppression. Thus, the attempt to forge a new identity born out of crime becomes an exhilarating experience. Their rebellious pride, which was the initial motivating force for violent action against an inferior other, is recast into a boastful arrogance. After disposing of wife and cat, the narrator of "The Black Cat" exults, "My happiness was supreme! The guilt of my dark deed disturbed me but little. . . . I soundly and tranquilly slept; aye, *slept* even with the burden of murder upon my soul" (605). "The burden of murder," however, proves eventually too heavy for these men to bear. From such pinnacles of momentary bravado, they descend into a realm of self-punishment that is narrated from within the lonely silence of the tomb, the jail, or the lunatic asylum.

In Poe's tales of homicide and revenge, the "spirit of perversity"—an unconscious urge toward self-destruction—helps to undercut the protagonist's criminal plan. Most of these tales reveal a desire to be caught or at least a need for self-punishment that is as strong or stronger than the urge toward violent crime and the attendant anarchy of its brief personal freedom. In both "The Tell-Tale Heart" and "The Black Cat," for example, the police arrive and stimulate a desire on the part of the narrator to confess his crime and undergo punishment from the state. In "The Masque of the Red Death" and "The Tell-Tale Heart," clock imagery is associated with the erosion of personal well-being and criminal design. As a symbol of reality's inevitable separation from the subjective fantasies of the human imagination, elements associated with time and clock imagery specifically in these stories help to undercut and eventually thwart the protagonist's effort to create a self-constructed world. Poe's characters commit their crimes and almost instantaneously activate some principle of judgment—both inside and outside the self. These tales of homicide often conclude with the understanding that the destruction of another human being results in the inevitable destruction of the self. If crime and criminal are inextricably linked in Poe, so are the elements of crime and self-punishment.

THE MASQUE OF THE RED DEATH (1842)

This tale was originally printed in *Graham's Magazine* for May 1842. A revised version appeared in the *Literary Souvenir* of June 4, 1842, with the title changed from *Mask* (1842) to *Masque* (1845). Yet another version of the tale was reprinted in the *Broadway Journal* of July 19, 1845.

SETTING AND PLOT

One of Poe's most colorful and visually pictorial narratives, the tale is set entirely in a castle belonging to Prince Prospero, a wealthy, powerful, and self-indulgent monarch. Outside the secluded abbey, the plague, here given the name the Red Death, ravages Prospero's kingdom to the point where "his dominions were half depopulated" (485). To avoid contamination, Prospero secures himself and a "thousand hale and light-hearted friends" (485) behind an enormous wall buttressed with gates of iron. Locked safely inside, the Prince and his cronies establish an exclusive and enclosed world of pleasure and perpetual revelry: "There were buffoons, there were improvisatori, there were ballet-dancers, there was Beauty, there was wine" (485).

During the five or six months of their seclusion, Prospero and his retinue continue to party steadily within the castle, a structure that consists of seven profusely decorated and multicolored chambers "so irregularly disposed that the vision embraced but little more than one at a time" (486). The seven rooms correspond to Shakespeare's seven ages of man and, ironically, to the seven stages of deadly sin culminating in the worst of sins, pride. The separate chambers, each completely decorated in a different color scheme, move from east (sunrise) to west (sunset), connected by a serpentine corridor. The most western of these rooms, however, is "shrouded in black velvet tapestries . . . but in this chamber only, the color of the windows failed to correspond with the decorations. The panes here were scarlet—a deep blood color" (486). This room also contains a giant ebony clock at whose chiming of the hour "it was observed that the giddiest grew pale" (487).

One evening, in his quest to pursue ever more lavish indulgences, Prospero hosts a "masked ball of the most unusual magnificence" (485). At the height of the party, an uninvited guest appears wearing a mask and costume meant to suggest the physical symptoms of contamination by the Red Death. Prospero demands that all the revelers unmask at midnight; when the interloper refuses, the enraged and insulted prince chases him through all the chambers of the castle, finally cornering him in the black chamber. There, "within the shadow of the ebony clock," the figure turns to face Prospero and reveals himself to be a ghost, "the grave-cerements and corpse-like mask . . . untenanted by any tangible form" (490). As the ebony clock finishes sounding the midnight chimes, each of the party guests, the prince included, falls to the ground "in the blood-bedewed halls of their revel, and died each in the despairing posture of his fall" (490). The Red Death "had come like a thief in the night" (490). The final paragraph of the story, paralleling the seven rooms in Prospero's abbey, contains seven pulsating clauses, each commencing with an "And," providing the rhythm of a clocklike measurement of doom.

CHARACTERS

Prince Prospero is named after Shakespeare's godlike creator of his own private and inviolable world in the play, *The Tempest*. Shakespeare's play centers upon a powerful man, Prospero, who transforms a primitive and barbaric island into a pastoral paradise. Like Poe's Prospero, Shakespeare's character creates an environment that corresponds to his vision of how the world should look. But Prospero's island is a precarious place; the beast-man Caliban represents the destructive energies of nature that continually threaten the reign of Prospero. Not only does Poe take his character's name from Shakespeare, but also the title for the story itself. In the first act of *The Tempest*, Caliban curses Prospero: "the red plague rid you" (1, 2, 364). Paralleling Shakespeare's play, Poe's main character learns that human efforts to avoid the hostile forces of nature (in the form of the plague) are doomed to failure. As Shakespeare's Prospero concedes his inability either to vanquish or elevate the wild Caliban, Poe's Prospero is likewise humbled in his encounter with nature's most vicious force in the figure of the Red Death itself. Poe's prince likewise closely resembles William Beckford's sensuous and self-indulgent monarch from the book *Vathek* (1786), a novel Poe read carefully and referenced in several other short stories.

Prospero reveals himself to be a man devoid of conscience or sympathy for his fellow man. While his kingdom languishes under the pestilence of the plague, Prospero locks himself and his closest friends inside a fortress where they will stay secluded until the plague has run its course. In addition to being protected from contamination, they feel free to indulge wildly decadent behavior: "[S]ecurity [was] within. . . . The external world could take care of itself" (485). The natural question that arises from these facts is why does Prospero behave in such a callous manner? Aside from obviously being a man immune to the sufferings of others, the prince also appears to be a sadist who enjoys his pleasures most thoroughly at the expense of others. He is the type of man who would gain great satisfaction—because it is a sign of his ultimate power—describing in detail the gourmet dinner he is digesting to a homeless person who has not had a decent meal in weeks.

Poe reminds us that the devastating and incurable effects of the Red Death, with its horrible "bleeding at the pores," isolates the victim "from the aid and from the sympathy of his fellow-men" (485). In the end, it is Prospero himself who is "shut out from the aid and sympathy" not only in his selfish pursuit of pleasure and arrogant exclusion, but in the very manner in which he dies: alone in the black room, face-to-face with death. He had sought in vain to isolate himself from death—the universal equalizer that we all share, regardless of social position, power, or amount of wealth. His own death mocks this very effort to insulate himself through both his self-imposed seclusion and feelings of superiority to his "fellow-men."

The lords and ladies who surround Prospero are fantastically costumed party fixtures. They flit through the apartments in the abbey searching for more alcohol or other stimulants, like spoiled, empty-headed revelers at a wedding someone else is paying for. Little wonder that Stephen King relied so heavily upon allusions to "The Masque of the Red Death" when he wished to create his own version of a perpetual party atmosphere at the Overlook Hotel in the novel *The Shining*.

If the perpetual party people in this tale are an impersonal collection of costumes, the figure of the Red Death, in contrast, is a highly individualized creation that certainly arrests the attention of reader as well as prince. It stands out immediately from the other party revelers, especially since its purpose is to mock Prospero in dressing in a costume identical to symptoms associated with the Red Death, and then to disobey his orders when it is time to unmask. In medieval art, it was customary for the specter of death to wear a version of the costume of his prey, and to mock with grotesque exaggeration the victim's behavior and/or daily activity. For the medieval artist, death is a double; Prince Prospero meets his own death in a kind of terrifying mirror, clothed in a costume that caricatures that part of himself he has tried so hard to deny.

The figure of the Red Death is likewise linked to the theme of devastating time so pronounced in many of Poe's tales of horror. Only the regular chiming of the ebony clock disrupts the fantasy realm contained within the sequestered abbey. The measured intrusion of reality signaling the passage of time each hour likewise signals the arrival of the Red Death, the ultimate destroyer of fantasy and symbol of reality. Like time itself, the Red Death possesses a kind of invisibility. Human beings remain unable to "grasp" it fully or to command it, but all are affected by its passage nonetheless. Its presence dissipates the self-contained atmosphere that Prospero has labored so hard to establish; his revelers are abruptly silenced in their hourly awareness of time's intrusive presence: "The dreams are stiff-frozen as they stand . . . the echoes of the chime die away"

(488). In this tale, time joins with the Red Death's "dominion over all," mocking Prospero's concerted efforts to circumvent death and the transience of human life.

THEMES

"The Masque of the Red Death" is an excellent illustration of Poe's thematic obsession with creating fantastic worlds of the imagination. Everything about this tale suggests a purely imaginative realm beyond the strictures of reality, and to some extent, the very act of this creation is a central theme of the narrative. Overwhelmed by images of elaborate swirling costumes, bejeweled masks adding to the allure and mystery of beautiful and privileged people, and a decadent environment of rich colors and sounds, the reader is transported into Prince Prospero's exclusive pleasure palace. It is a realm that resembles a dream-fantasy, music video, or exotic night club more than a realist representation of everyday life.

Yet, in the midst of creating this exciting fantastical enterprise, Poe's third-person omniscient narrative voice hesitates to inform us that even though "[t]here was much of the beautiful, much of the wanton, much of the *bizarre.* and something of the terrible" surrounding the construction of this artificial world, there was also "not a little of that which might have excited disgust" (487–88). Surely the last part of this authorial commentary is meant as a judgment on Prince Prospero's self-indulgence. But it seems likewise a critique of the story's emphasis on pure *excess*, of individuals who have lost sight of reality in the confusion of an intoxicating fog. Poe, who was never one for moderation in either his own drinking or self-indulgent behavior, understood, perhaps better than most people, the attraction of such an environment. And yet, by 1842, he had also learned that such self-indulgences came at a heavy price, that what often appears to be real—whether it be the glitterati of Prospero's abbey, or the perspective induced by a brain immersed in alcohol—is in reality a dangerous illusion that often results in death. Thus, the theme of this tale culminates in two stern moral lessons: that the wages of sin is death, especially when that sin takes its shape in an arrogance that sets itself apart from the rest of humanity; and that prolonged exposure to the realm of excess eventually concludes in the loss of our tenuous hold on reality.

THE TELL-TALE HEART (1843)

Certainly one of the most famous and frequently anthologized of Poe's works, this short story was first published in the Boston periodical, *Pioneer*, for January 1843 and was later reprinted in the *Dollar Newspaper* of January 25, 1843. A revised version appeared in the *Broadway Journal* of August 23, 1843.

SETTING AND PLOT

Similar to so many of Poe's tales of horror, the setting of this story is absolutely removed from historical time and geographical place. It takes place entirely in the interior of an old house where a nameless narrator recalls how he conceived the idea of killing an old man. Although this narrator claims to be totally sane, he admits that there never existed a real motive for murder; it was just that the old man's eye vexed him: "Object there was none. Passion there was none. I loved the old man. . . . I think it was his eye! Yes, it was this! One of his eyes resembles that of a vulture—a pale blue eye with a film over it" (555).

The first half of the story details the narrator's nightly ritual of spying upon the old man sleeping. For a week before the crime he crept into the man's bedroom to shine the light of a lantern upon the eye. On the eighth night, the narrator tipped the bed over on his victim and smothered him. He then meticulously dismembered the body, hiding its various parts under the floor planking, euphoric that he has managed to catch all the blood in a pail. However, soon after completing the task of hiding the body, as the bell signaled four o'clock in the morning, "there came a knocking at the street door. . . . There entered three men, who introduced themselves, with perfect suavity, as officers of the police" (558). At first, the murderer is confident that he has done his work well; he even goes so far as to invite the police to sit in the room where the body is buried, "while I myself, in the wild audacity of my perfect triumph, placed my own seat upon the very spot beneath which reposed the corpse of the victim" (559).

As the narrator concocts a lie explaining to the police that the old man is out of town, he begins to develop a strong headache, feels himself going pale, and appears less confident in his attitude and speech. What he imagines to be the pulsations of the old man's heart, a sound that resembled "*a low, dull, quick sound—much such a sound as a watch makes when enveloped in cotton*" (559), begins to grow ever louder in the confines of the narrator's head. The sound causes him to scream out his guilt to the police and to indicate the location of the victim. The police apparently cannot hear this sound. The narrator claims it exists outside his head, but by the end of the story we know that it is inside his mind and being projected outward. Its enlarged presence inside his own head compels him to confess in hopes that this will alleviate the presence and pressure of the heart's beating.

CHARACTERS

The narrator in this story makes the claim so strongly for his sanity—"why *will* you say that I am mad?" (555)—that the reader is immediately suspicious. His attempts to distance himself from insanity, to prove himself sane, succeed only in focusing the reader's attention upon his unstable mental condition.

From the opening lines to the end, the narrator demonstrates that he is meticulous, obsessed, a fetishist, and quite out of his mind. How else to explain the post-operative resonance of a heart that refuses to die and his rationale for murder: a vulturelike eye. The narrator's truest fascination for the reader is to be found in his duplicity. He can boast of his preparations to make sure that the blood does not splatter when dismembering the corpse and smile charmingly as he reports to the police that it was his own screams at midnight that awakened the neighbor. On the other hand, his excitement is so profound that he can barely hide the old man's body. In the end, the narrator is pursued by the violence and anguish of his own actions, and ultimately fails in his efforts to project it outward away from himself.

The old man in this tale exists as little more than a collection of body parts. He has no voice in the narrative, except for a late-night groan of terror and the single shriek that he utters at the very moment of his death. And yet, while he exerts no real vocal presence in the tale, we are sharply aware, through the acute senses of the narrator, of the *internal* workings of his body: his beating heart, the blood racing through his veins, the old man's mental "terror [that] must have been extreme!" (557). We know as well that the man has money, that he is afraid of robbers, and that one of his eyes is filmed over by a cataract. Perhaps he is also confined to his bedroom because of other ailments. In any event, his midnight nightmares come to life in the actions of his housemate, made even more terrifying when we consider that the murderer professes to "love" his victim.

The police who arrive at four in the morning appear to be very sleepy, indeed. They sit "chatting of familiar things" (559), are satisfied with both the narrator's explanations and "manner," and apparently do not notice either the growing anxiety of the murderer or his madness (other than the paperboy, who chats "cheerily" at four in the morning?). The revelation of this crime may come as little surprise to a reader who has watched the slow splintering of the narrator's mind, but one can presume that the police are utterly shocked. This portrait of the police as totally ineffectual when coping with criminal deception will be of great importance to the next chapter's examination of the role of the detective as superior to the procedures of the police.

THEMES

"The Tell-Tale Heart" has definitely earned its reputation as a classic narrative of a mind's psychological unraveling. One can immediately see why this narrative, with its attention to violence that is first perpetrated upon a victim, only to then be turned upon the victimizer, held such significance for writers like Feodor Dostoevski and filmmakers like Alfred Hitchcock. In this ultimate Gothic story of a self trapped within the dungeon of its own half-understood impulses, the senses deprive the mind of choice—"anything was better than this agony!"—and the narrator is compelled to "scream or die" (559). The decision on the part of the narrator to act upon his murderous impulses sets in motion an inextricable identification between victim and victimizer. Just prior to the murder, as the old man sits rigidly in his bed, heart pounding, the narrator anticipates and parallels his every move: "I did not hear him lie down. He was still sitting up in the bed listening—just as I have done, night after night, hearkening to the death watches in the wall" (556). As the narrator spends a week preparing himself to commit the crime, he forms a bond with the old man, acknowledging that the victim's terror of death is likewise shared by the man who will bring death into the bedchamber: "Many a night, just a midnight, when all the world slept, [terror] has welled up from my own bosom, deepening, with its dreadful echo, the terrors that distracted me. I say I knew it well. I knew what the old man felt, and pitied him" (556).

This evolving bond between murderer and the murdered is very important to recognize because it helps to explain why the narrator is compelled to confess his crime mere hours after its execution. From the second paragraph of the tale it is clear that the "eye" of the old man is meant to be juxtaposed symbolically with the first-person narrative "I" of the storyteller. Notice the way in which Poe's syntax blurs the "eye-I" distinction in the following sentences: "For his gold I had no desire. I think it was his eye! Yes, it was this! One of his eyes resembled that of a vulture—a pale blue eye, with a film over it. Whenever it fell upon me, my blood ran cold; and so by degrees—very gradually—I made up my mind to take the life of the old man, and thus rid myself of the eye for ever" (555).

Indeed, the identities of the old man and narrator run together in the act of murder itself: the killer's yell is amplified by the old man's simultaneous shriek. By the end of the tale the narrator is living inside the old man's bloodstream, the old man's heart is beating inside the narrator's head. This condition is not literal, of course, but rather psychological—brought on by the murderer's inability to separate himself from the person he has murdered. Lacking any clear sense of inner vision, the murderer learns about himself only by living through the old man. And the fact that he kills this man suggests that the focus of the narrator's violence is not really upon the vulture "eye," but rather the "I" of self-consciousness that has been projected upon the old man. By killing the old man, in other words, the narrator is attempting to kill a part of himself.

After the crime, the sound of the old man's heart grows in intensity and volume, and both increase as a direct response to the narrator's efforts at distancing himself from the old man by first burying him under the floor and then lying to the police that his victim is "absent in the country" (558). While the narrator initially experienced a sense of triumph in the act of killing, immediately afterwards this euphoria is transformed into horror as it becomes impossible for narrator and reader alike to distinguish whose heart is actually beating—the old man's or the narrator's. The inability to make this distinction emphasizes both the extent that the old man is a mirror for the narrator and the level of madness that contributes to the murderer's self-destruction.

As evinced in the tale "The Masque of the Red Death," midnight is often the hour at which crime and supernatural events occur in Poe. The raised clock hands symbolize both the triumph of the murderer's will and the suspension of time in the momentary limbo of what is neither today, yesterday, nor tomorrow. But no sooner does an individual consciousness reach this state of moral suspension than his own self-punishment commences. Just as the upraised hands of the clock signaling the midnight hour must eventually separate, the murderer feels compelled to undermine his own efforts. The darkness of night gives way to the light of morning. Once more, as in "The Masque of the Red Death," the animated clock becomes an objective signifier of the real world, a constant reminder of powerful forces that exist outside the control of the individual's will thwarting his efforts to create an idealized mental state. In "The Tell-Tale Heart," the murderer is eventually stalked by images of time as he, in turn, stalks his victim. The tale these hearts tell is connected to the heart's beating, a syncopated measurement of time: each beat denotes another lost moment in time where the heart is that much closer to running out of time.

It is midnight when the criminal approaches the old man, the vigil of watching him sleep lasts an hour, and this procedure takes place every night for a week. On the eighth night, the murder is committed by a man who moved slower than "a watch's minute hand" (556), the police arrive precisely at four o'clock, while the old man's beating heart haunts the narrator's psyche with the "*sound as a watch makes when enveloped in cotton*" (559). Having closed the annoying vulture-eye, the narrator is assailed by the infernal pulsations of the old man's body clock—measuring the time the narrator has left before he must confess, the time he has left before being taken to jail, the time he has left inhabiting the world of the sane. Thus, a major theme in this story revolves around a narrator who initially manipulates time imagery as a means for torturing his victim and even manages to regulate time itself (at least in his own head). By the conclusion of the tale, however, he has lost control over these images as they are turned against him and used to suggest the clock's (and reality's) remorseless progress and its ruinous effects upon the individual will.

THE BLACK CAT (1843)

This tale was originally published on the front page of the Philadelphia *Saturday Evening Post* of August 19, 1843. Poe was a cat lover, and owned several during his lifetime, including a bright black cat named Caterrina. He was especially fond of feline companionship while writing. No reader of Poe should confuse the feline sadism of the narrator of "The Black Cat" with Poe's deep and genuine affection for these animals.

SETTING AND PLOT

The story is narrated by a man who is in jail awaiting his execution for murder that is scheduled for the next day. Thus, the tale is a final confession. Aside from the writer's jail cell, the rest of the tale takes place in the narrator's house situated in an unknown city. Early on we learn of the narrator's love of animals. He and his wife kept many different kinds of pets, including a black cat named Pluto. This harmonious domestic scene began to change with the introduction of alcohol into the narrator's life. As his addiction deepened, his personality became more aggressive: "I grew, day by day, more moody, more irritable, more regardless of the feelings of others. . . . At length, I even offered my wife personal violence" (598). One night he returned home intoxicated, seized Pluto, and cut out one of his eyes. Once sobered, he was filled with a terrible sense of remorse, but of course the maimed cat was now wary of him. Pluto's efforts to avoid the narrator only aroused the latter's wrath, and eventually he hangs the cat from a tree next to the house. That evening, he and his wife are left homeless. On the one remaining wall next to his bedroom the gigantic figure of a cat with a rope around its neck is left imprinted, like a giant stage prop.

Months pass and the narrator's problem with alcohol deepens. One night, drunk in a tavern, he finds another cat that resembles Pluto even to the point of a missing eye. The narrator takes the feline to his new home where his wife bonds with it immediately. Perhaps because of his earlier experience with Pluto, or perhaps because his wife forms such a deep attachment to it, the narrator's feelings toward this second cat quickly deteriorate: "The moodiness of my usual temper increased to hatred of all things and all mankind; while, from the sudden, frequent, and ungovernable outbursts of a fury to which I now abandoned myself, my uncomplaining wife, alas! Was the most usual and most patient of sufferers" (603). One day while working in the basement he almost trips over the cat, and this sparks in him the urge to kill the animal. He swings an axe at it, but his wife intervenes to stop his arm. Furious at her interference, "into a rage more than demoniacal, I withdrew my arm from her grasp and buried the axe in her brain. She fell dead upon the spot, without a groan" (603). The next several paragraphs of the tale detail the narrator's attempt to conceal the corpse. In the cellar he removes part of a wall and inters his wife's body; he then repositions the wall so that it appears as if it has not been touched.

Four days after the crime, the police come to investigate the wife's disappearance. Confident in his efforts at concealment and feeling only a little bit guilty, the narrator feels a sudden "phrenzy of bravado" and raps upon "that very portion of the brick-work upon which stood the corpse of the wife of my bosom" (605). A sound from within the wall emerges immediately as if in answer to his tapping, "a wailing shriek, half of horror and half of triumph, such as might have arise only out of hell" (606). Instead of leaving, the police tear down the wall and upon the head of the decomposing wife is the missing black cat, "with red extended mouth and solitary eye of fire" (606).

CHARACTERS

The narrator is a man in crisis. His drinking has pushed him to the point where he is capable of violence, even against a wife who, although patient and long-suffering, is incapable of helping her husband. The two cats in this story remind him of better days, before the narrator's alcoholism produced in his personality "a radical alteration for the worst" (598). But his substance abuse has provided him with at least one insight. He has learned that "the spirit of PERVERSENESS," the self's "unfathomable longing to *vex itself*—to offer violence to its own nature," is a fundamental aspect of "the character of Man" (599). The narrator's alcoholism, his propensity for violent behavior, his acute isolation, and his volatile temper are all characteristics of *perverseness*: that is, they are reflective of self-destructive behavior. Moreover, his desire to punish and abuse both wife and cats, with whom he maintains ambivalent love-hate feelings, highlights the narrator's internal sickness. He is a man who lacks psychological balance. On the one hand, he claims that the murder of his wife "disturbed me but little. . . . I looked upon my future felicity as secured" (605). On the other hand, the concluding scene with the police must be read in light of the speaker's desire for further self-punishment: much like the narrator in "The Tell-Tale Heart," he pounds on the wall to call attention to his crime, to put himself in a position where he can exorcise his own self-contempt.

The black cats in this tale possess certain supernal qualities that certainly confound the narrator. In the 1840 essay "Instinct vs Reason—A Black Cat," Poe speculates that feline intuition is in many instances superior to human reason, and he offers as evidence his own cat's ability to unlock door latches with her cunning paws. The narrator's wife in "The Black Cat" "made frequent allusion to the ancient popular notion, which regarded all black cats as witches in disguise" (598). The first cat is named Pluto, the Greek name for the king of hell, or hell itself. And while the second cat has no name, the image of its red mouth and fiery eye at the end of this story is suggestive of an infernal presence. It is not that these cats are creatures sent from the underworld to torment the narrator so much as the animals become reflections of the narrator's own inner hell, his self-torment. They embody the speaker's rage and egotism, as well as his perverse urge toward self-destruction.

THEMES

The cats in this tale are also closely aligned with the narrator's wife. Not only does she love and protect them from her husband's wrath, the second cat returns her loyalty in thwarting the narrator's attempt to get away with murder. The two cats and the wife herself represent those feminine characteristics in himself that the narrator has systematically repressed: sensitivity, domestic tranquility, a concern and respect for animals and other people, and an appreciation for life in general. Poe's protagonist wallows in gin to create a world of dark indulgence. He is, like many of Poe's male protagonists, an extremely selfish man who seeks desperately to be at the center of an alcoholic universe of his own making. His wife, like his domestic pets, is merely part of a disposable world—one of his possessions. But the problem for the narrator in "The Black Cat" is that his wife simply refuses to abide by his design; she is a woman, like the cats she resembles and admires, who is neither predictable nor easily dominated (e.g., she dares to stop his hand when he wishes to destroy his pet). Poe appears to imply in this cat tale that a man's love for a woman is closely aligned to a human's relationship with a cat: the harder a human seeks to force his will upon a cat, especially through violent abuse, the less likely he is to inspire feline affection or loyalty. The cats and wife in this tale represent feminine principles, perhaps akin to life itself, that when either thwarted or violently repressed only lead to male self-destruction.

As much as this tale contains themes about male antipathy toward women, it is also a story that confronts the thematic issue of alcoholism and the destructive effects that it produces upon domestic life. When the narrator confesses that "my disease grew upon me—for what disease is like Alcohol" (598), he is echoing a sentiment that Poe himself understood intimately. While sober, Poe was like the narrator in his earlier, happier days: kind and loving. But alcohol produced in both men a tendency toward violence and aggressive behavior. Poe's alcoholism not only cost him friendships and important connections because of his tendency to quarrel violently with others, he also spent time in jail for public drunkenness. In creating the narrator in "The Black Cat," Poe invested him with many of his own character flaws while drunk; the narrator is not meant to be Poe himself, but Poe used many of the particulars of his own experience in rendering the narrator's personality.

THE IMP OF THE PERVERSE (1845)

Initially published in the July 1845 issue of *Graham's Magazine*, this short story is an odd combination of elements of the confessional murder narrative and the philosophical essay.

SETTING AND PLOT

One of Poe's shortest stories, the narrative is nearly split in half—the first dealing with a philosophical rumination of the theory of *perverseness*, and the second the actual history of the narrator, who is awaiting execution for a murder to which he has confessed. The story itself is narrated, as in "The Black Cat," from the enclosed confines of a jail cell, but the murder itself takes place in the bedroom of a man whose estate the narrator wishes to inherit.

The concept of perversity, as the narrator describes it, is the "strongly antagonistical sentiment" (828) of human beings to perform self-destructive acts. When reason exerts its influence, we are capable of masterful actions, remaining always in control of ourselves. But at the same time as reason guides us forward, the tendency to wreck everything we have accomplished—or perversity—is also present working against our every effort. "Our reason deters us from the brink of a precipice . . . [perversity] meditates a plunge" (829).

After exploring these two contradictory sides of human behavior, the narrator sets out to illustrate his theory. For months he has "pondered upon the means of murdering" (830) his victim. He rejected many schemes because each involved the risk of detection. Finally, through the implementation of reason, he came up with the perfect plan. After reading some French memoirs, the narrator discovered an account of a death that occurred as a result of a poisoned candle that resulted in the accidental suffocation of a person who was in the room breathing its vapors. Constructing such a candle himself, the narrator succeeds in killing his victim, and immediately inherits his fortune.

For years the narrator lived with neither guilt nor public suspicion. He sauntered the streets of an American city pondering his security and reveling in his accomplishment. But one day perversity struck: "I arrested myself in the act of murmuring, half aloud, 'I am safe—I am safe—yes—if I be not fool enough to make open confession!' " (831). From this point forward, reason abandoned the narrator, and he began to behave "like a madman bounding through the crowded thoroughfares" (831). Unable to maintain control over the urge to confess, it was as though "some invisible fiend struck me with his broad palm upon the back. The long imprisoned secret burst forth from my soul" (831). His confession results in a conviction for murder that "consigned me to the hangman, and to hell" (831).

CHARACTERS

The narrator lectures scientifically on "the Imp of the Perverse," (830), arguing that all human beings are split in two between the desire to gratify their secret urges and the need to be punished for these desires. As he wanders the streets of the city, it is not clear whether the narrator wants to call attention to his crime because he is proud of his cleverness and wants to proclaim it to others, or because he is motivated by a more deliberate attempt to bring about his own self-destruction. In either case, the imp-narrator makes it clear that the desire for self-punishment does not necessarily concern guilt or the need to receive justice from an authority figure. Instead, confession occurs when the criminal realizes the perverse pleasure involved in actively dooming himself, because he knows full well that he should not open his mouth, and the imp cannot be gratified until others are made aware of his crime. As further illustrated in "The Cask of Amontillado," "The Tell-Tale Heart," and "The Black Cat," there can be no real satisfaction in the commission of a crime unless the criminal can tell someone about the deed. This is the way many crimes are solved by police even today: the criminal eventually cannot resist revealing his secret to somebody, and then it is no longer a secret.

THEMES

By demonstrating the discomforting psychological truth that human beings are often driven by self-destructive impulses, "The Imp of the Perverse" posits a basis for understanding the irrational deeds of many Poe narrators, such as the compulsive characters in "The Tell-Tale Heart" and "The Black Cat." In fact, any student interested in understanding fully why so many of Poe's murderers are drawn to seemingly irrational acts of confession and consequent punishment, despite elaborate efforts to keep from getting caught, must be familiar with the theory of perversity as it is used in "The Imp of the Perverse." Perverseness is for Poe a fascinating paradox, for it is the unreasonable counterpoint to security and self-protection; it suggests that human beings are drawn to their own self-destruction. Certainly Poe's many fictional illustrations of perversity underscore explanations for why people continue to drink excessively and practice unsafe sex with strangers despite the abundant medical proof that both may cause serious health complications, or why so many of us are drawn back repetitively into relationships with partners who are either chronically abusive or pathologically manipulative.

THE CASK OF AMONTILLADO (1846)

This short story was initially published in *Godey's Lady's Book* for November 1846. The tale of revenge may possess certain autobiographical resonances, as Poe desired to punish the anonymous author—later revealed to be Charles F. Briggs, editor of the *Broadway Journal*—who slandered Poe in a May 26, 1846, article published in the New York *Evening Mirror*. The article had censured

Poe's drinking and mocked his physical appearance. Poe was enraged by the piece and subsequently won more than $200 in a lawsuit. Whatever part of the insult that remained unsatisfied by a monetary enumeration may have been worked out in this tale of revenge.

SETTING AND PLOT

The tale opens during "the supreme madness of the carnival season" (848), which is important for several reasons. First, everyone is elaborately costumed and masked, helping to create, as in "The Masque of the Red Death," an atmosphere of licentious freedom. The Roman Catholic carnival season, or Mardi Gras, as it is known in the United States, is a period just before the start of Lent when revelers engage in wild behavior before the restrictions of Lent go into effect. In this party environment, Montressor meets Fortunato on an Italian street and entices him home to his wine cellar in order to ascertain whether or not Montressor is in possession of an authentic cask of expensive Amontillado sherry. Although feeling under the weather, Fortunato's pride refuses him to allow Montressor to seek the opinion of another connoisseur; he must be the one to taste and judge the wine.

The rest of the tale is the journey that these two men take as they make their descent into Montressor's expansive underground wine cellar. On the way, we learn that Fortunato is "rich, respected, admired, beloved" (850), happy, as Montressor once was before he was terribly wronged at the hands of Fortunato himself. Fortunato has no awareness that he has insulted such a deadly foe; he follows Montressor deeper into the vault, accepting drinks from a bottle of Medoc that Montressor supplies along the way, and even joining in a toast to his long life.

Soon the two reach a small cul-de-sac at the end of a corridor littered with the bones of Montressor's ancestors. There, Montressor surprises Fortunato by securing him to the back wall with chains bolted to the wall itself. Once Fortunato is immobilized, Montressor begins the work of sealing him between two stone layers by carefully building a wall directly in front of his victim. At first, Fortunato thinks this is all part of a joke—"We will have many a rich laugh about it at the palazzo" (854)—but as the rows of mortar grow higher, and the darkness increases within the limited space that is left to him, the cruel revenge that Montressor is exacting becomes terrifyingly real. As Montressor slides the final stone into place, Fortunato begs for mercy with a cry: "*For the love of God, Montressor!*" (854), only to be mocked by his murderer who echoes, "Yes, for the love of God" (854), and then exits, leaving Fortunato to a slow death in the crypt.

CHARACTERS

Fortunato appears to be an important and cultured man in his social circle. His name means "the fortunate man," an ironic twist given the fact that it remains his supreme misfortune to have wronged a man with a deathless memory and a commitment to "not only punish, but punish with impunity" (848). We never learn the exact offense Fortunato has committed, and thus can make no evaluation upon whether Montressor's revenge is justifiable. But the fact that he is unaware of the extent of Montressor's need for revenge suggests that either Fortunato is extremely naïve or Montressor is a very cunning criminal. Both of these are probably true. Poe purposely dresses Fortunato in the suit of a clown to join in the celebration of carnival. Fortunato's ability to assess and judge situations accurately is severely called into question at the beginning of the story when he insists upon leaving his family and friends to descend into a damp wine vault in order to answer Montressor's challenge at judging the worth of a cask of wine. His pride is so great that he feels he alone is capable of making this evaluation; he pays a terrible price for this arrogance.

Montressor is similar to many of Poe's murderers: coolly rational on the surface but raging inside. His need to exact revenge upon Fortunato sharpens his obsessive nature to the point where the moral implications of his actions become insignificant compared to the supreme satisfaction he receives from punishing his adversary. Montressor is perhaps the best illustration in all of literature of the adage, "Revenge is a dish best served cold," meaning that the longer the wait of anticipating and planning revenge, the deeper the satisfaction when it finally takes place. Behind the carefully constructed mask of friendship and concern, he lures Fortunato to a death that reflects perfectly Montressor's cynical genius. Without his employing guns or other weapons, his victim will either suffocate or die from starvation and is likely to go insane in either case. Fortunato's final demise will be slow and terrible, as he will be conscious of his helplessness to the very end.

THEMES

"The Cask of Amontillado" is another of Poe's first-person narratives told from the point of view of a monster. The theme of this story, like so many of Poe's horror tales, reveals an obsessive person who has spent the best of his life's energies first planning and then executing the calculated murder of another person. Fifty years later, Montressor is still thinking about the corpse that has been quietly rotting in the corner of his wine cellar. A deluded rationalist who convinces himself that he will find consummate satisfaction in revenging himself upon his enemy, Montressor emerges, as literary critic James Gargano argues, as "both a compulsive and pursued man; for in committing a flawless crime against another human being, he really commits the worst of crimes against himself" (180). While Montressor, like the narrator of "The Tell-Tale Heart," exalts in an ironic appreciation of his own vile design, the careful reader notes well that at the ultimate moment of his triumph over Fortunato, just as he is about to leave him alone for eternity in his dark stone tomb, Montressor hears a faint, pathetic "jingling of the bells" from Fortunato's carnival costume. While Montressor claims that his "heart grew sick [upon hearing the sound]—on account of the dampness of the catacombs" (854), it is interesting that this is the first time he has mentioned such a sentiment during the long walk to this underground spot. Moreover, the fact that he then "hastened to make an end of my labor" (854) implies that his earlier arrogant zeal has perhaps been complicated by the reality of an imminent murder. His haste to leave the scene of the crime stands in direct contrast to the initial complacency with which he savors both the telling of his story and the fettering of Fortunato to the back of a wall.

As in "The Black Cat" and "The Tell-Tale Heart," this story is a confession of sorts. After fifty years of keeping this dark history a secret, walling it up within his own heart, Montressor is compelled finally to write it down, to bring his crime out into the light. When he tells us at the end of the tale that "[f]or the half of a century no mortal has disturbed" (854) the stone wall and surrounding bones that hide Fortunato, the concern must shift from Montressor's motivation for killing his enemy, to his motivation for telling us the story itself. Although it is clear that Montressor plainly enjoys the retelling of this ritualized memorial reenactment of the "immolation" of his drunken rival, it is also true that he has been carrying the memory of this crime inside him for fifty years. He is now an old man, perhaps making a final confession. Never totally out of his memory, the murderous deed has become the obsession of his life; the truest part of his existence resides underground, in the tomb where he has buried both his enemy—and, symbolically, his own soul.

"The Cask of Amontillado" blends a wonderfully macabre sense of humor with a deep element of irony (or, a surprising change from what is expected) throughout. As the two men proceed along toward Fortunato's ultimate resting place, Montressor's sarcastic commentary and behavior—from toasting his victim's health and long life, to revealing his mason trowel when Fortunato mentions that he is a member of the secret Mason society, to toying with the chained Fortunato by telling him that he intends to provide him "all the little attentions in my power" (852)—makes this one of Poe's darkest comedies. It reflects the humor of a mind tickled by its own perversity. But the narrative's ultimate irony is perhaps reserved for Montressor himself, who naïvely trusted that he would find an everlasting peace in revenging an insult he could neither forget nor forgive. While the story may have had as its intention the narrative of Montressor's punishment with impunity, it is really Fortunato who has for the past fifty years continued to punish Montressor, if only as a dead memory from which he is never wholly free.

"HOP-FROG" (1849)

First published in *The Flag of Our Union* on March 17, 1849, this short story, one of the last that Poe would write, was then titled "Hop-Frog; Or, The Eight Chained Ourang-outangs." One certain source for this tale of revenge appeared in a passage quoted from the chronicles of the French medieval historian Jean Froissart and reprinted in the *Broadway Journal* of February 1, 1845, that described a fire and homicide in the court of Charles VI.

SETTING AND PLOT

Unusual for Poe's normal narrative point of view, the tale is told through an innocent-eyed spectator, who describes, in fairy-tale-like language, a king whose greatest contribution appears to be his love of jokes. Set in a mythical kingdom in the distant past, this king lives in a large castle, unmarried, with seven ministers who advise and cater to the king's various whims. Additionally, because of the king's penchant for practical jokes, the castle is equipped with two dwarfs, Hop-Frog and Trippetta, who play the roles of court jesters or fools to entertain the king and his ministers at various court gatherings. Hop-Frog's "value was trebled in the eyes of the king, by the fact of his being also a dwarf and a cripple" (899).

On a grand state occasion, the king decides to have a masquerade party, and summons Hop-Frog to help plan a spectacular joke. To satisfy the king's craving for "something novel" (901), Hop-Frog is commissioned to come up with an unusual prank. At first the dwarf is reluctant to contribute, as he is accustomed to being humiliated by these efforts to entertain the insensitive king. To encourage his involvement, the king forces Hop-Frog to drink wine until he is drunk. His intoxication combined with an episode of violence against Trippetta (the king throws a goblet of wine in her face and pushes her roughly away from him) inspire Hop-Frog to an idea. He proposes putting the king and his ministers into tight-fitting costumes soaked with tar and covered with flax. The joke will be to make them resemble ourang-outangs, or apes, "the resemblance so striking that the company of masqueraders will take you for real beasts—and of course, they will be as much terrified as astonished" (904). The king is delighted with this proposal, and compliments Hop-Frog with the insult, "[T]his is exquisite . . . I will make a man of you" (904).

On the night of the party, Hop-Frog leads the costumed king and his ministers into the castle's grand saloon—a circular room with a very high ceiling, the only natural light source a single window at the top. To increase the realism of his masquerade, Hop-Frog extends a length of chain connecting each man's waist, and brings them into the crowded room just after the clock chimes midnight. The attired creatures perform according to expectations: the other guests are so terrified that they try to escape the chamber. But the king had ordered the doors to be locked immediately upon his entrance. Amidst all the confusion and dismay, the king and his ministers are led by Hop-Frog, who holds a single end of the chain that connects and circles the men together, into the center of the room. Facing them, Hop-Frog gives a signal and the entire entourage is suddenly hauled thirty feet off the ground, suspended from a single chain attached to the ceiling. The agile dwarf, who has also ridden aloft upon the king's shoulders, pretends to wonder aloud who these creatures are. He thrusts a flaming torch close to the dangling king, whereupon recognizing "what manner of people these maskers are" (908), proceeds to set the eight men on fire. As the tar and flax combust fiercely, Hop-Frog scampers up the ceiling chain and vanishes through the single hole in the roof while "the eight corpses swung in their chains, a fetid, blackened, hideous, and indistinguishable mass" (908).

CHARACTERS

Nicknamed Hop-Frog because of his limp and diminutive size, he has been humiliated and sadistically mocked by the king and his ministers during his forced employment in the castle. Because Hop-Frog is both a foreigner and handicapped, the king has decided he is a worthy addition to his collection of bizarre and grotesque vehicles for inciting humor. His status as an outsider—he has been kidnapped from "some barbarous region that no person ever heard of" (900)—makes it impossible for him to run away or to object to the king's tyrannical treatment. However, it is clear almost immediately that he is much more than just a good-natured fool who entertains the selfish king. Hop-Frog seethes quietly throughout the tale; his continual habit of grinding his teeth indicates the level of fury and frustration he secretly harbors. The fact that Hop-Frog "was by no means popular" (900) suggests that others around him are wary of his growing fury even as they continue to make use of him as an object of derision.

Trippetta, in contrast to Hop-Frog, is a beautiful dwarf, and appears to be both the one person Hop-Frog respects in the castle and the impetus to motivate his rebellion against the king. It is one thing for the king to humiliate Hop-Frog, quite another when he goes after the lovely Trippetta. Because of her grace and exquisite beauty, Trippetta "possessed much influence; and never failed to use it, whenever she could, for the benefit of Hop-Frog" (900). Her gentle nature and unselfish devotion help to humanize Hop-Frog and motivate him to concoct an escape plan for them both, even if it does require the murders of their oppressors.

The king and his ministers consider themselves men of humor. But their particular brand of comedy always requires an object of ridicule, a target not so much "to laugh *with* . . . as to laugh *at*" (899). Often in Poe, individuals who get their laughs at the expense of others are destined for a severity of punishment that is anything but funny. In contrast to the severely deformed Hop-Frog, the king is described as corpulent, but also a "capital figure" (900). He is rich, good-looking, powerful, and, at least in his own fashion, possesses a large sense of humor. Like most bullies, however, he uses these attributes with which he has been blessed not to help others but to oppress them. In part, this strengthens his own sense of self-importance at the same time as it is a constant reminder to others that they must be careful to speak and act in a pleasing manner. Although quick to laugh, the king is not a kind man: "Over-niceties wearied him" (899). In fact, his obsession with practical jokes that come at the expense of another's dignity are merely a thin disguise for the basic cruelty that represents the king's core.

THEMES

This story closely resembles several other Poe tales that focus on ingenious and well-deserved revenge as well as the human-into-beast theme. Three earlier stories in particular, "The Cask of Amontillado," "Four Beasts in One," and "The System of Doctor Tarr and Professor Fether," have scenic and thematic connections with "Hop-Frog." Poe appears to have been rather attracted to the literary conceptualization of man-into-ape. In part, his interest stemmed from a desire to create offensively grotesque human-beast amalgamations that are meant to be both hideous and humorous, similar to the special effect creations a modern audience finds in many science-fiction films such as *Star Wars*. But Poe also employed the man-to-beast motif to underscore the essential theme of the story itself: human cruelty that instigates ingenious revenge.

The king is originally presented with Hop-Frog and Trippetta as exotic toys to stimulate his depraved sense of humor. As captive foreigners, the dwarfs are subject to inhumane treatment, and Hop-Frog is so named because of his repulsive deformity. The king and his court view the two dwarfs as subhuman beasts and therefore as objects of ridicule. But in reality, Hop-Frog and Trippetta genuinely love one another and their mutual concern for each other's welfare goes beyond a shared desire to survive their abuse at the hands of the king. The king claims that he "will make a man" (904) out of Hop-Frog, but the latter is already a man—the king has just failed to appreciate this fact. Whereas Hop-Frog is enslaved and treated with brutal scorn, he is actually the heroic man, inventing an escape plan that is both ingenious and darkly ironic. The king, on the other hand, who thinks of himself as a paragon of civility, is really an insensitive beast; he emerges as the truly repulsive character in this tale. Thus Hop-Frog's choice of placing him in the ape suit is merely an ironic externalization of the king's true nature. The beauty of Hop-Frog's inventive masquerade lies in the fact that the other masqueraders take the king and his advisors for the reality they depict.

Pushed to the point where the king crosses a line in humiliating his friend Trippetta, Hop-Frog devises a revenge that will literally make monkeys out of his tormentors and allowed him to have the last laugh as he escapes from his enforced captivity in the cruel court. His revenge is the ultimate punishment reserved for a bully, as the end of the tale reverses the power positionings established in the first half of the story. From the moment he suspends them from the ceiling of the grand saloon, the dwarf controls the fate of the king and his ministers; they dangle helplessly as literal marionettes, abruptly aware that Hop-Frog's "novel" joke has come at their own expense. As "practical jokes suited [the king's] taste far better than verbal ones" (899), Hop-Frog's choice of a royal flambé ironically incorporates the same admixture of black comedy and physical humiliation that underscores the king's own particular brand of humor. At the end of these tales of murder and revenge, the reader is caught between a contrasting visceral shudder and a genuine appreciation for Poe's imaginative choice of punishments.

ALTERNATIVE READING: MARXIST INTERPRETATION

Marxism is a particular ideology (political philosophy) that adheres to the teachings of German social critic and philosopher Karl Marx (1818–83). There probably exists no contemporary theoretical approach to literary studies that is more controversial than a Marxist analysis. After all, didn't the late 1980s collapse of communism as it was practiced in the Soviet Union signal the death knell of Marxism and the ascendency of its archenemy, capitalism?

In both *The Communist Manifesto* (1848) and the later book *Capital* (1867), Marx argued that capitalists, or the bourgeoisie, had enslaved the working class, or the proletariat, through economic exploitation. Only through a radical overthrow of this system could workers hope to better their oppressed status. A revolution must occur to strip the capitalists of their money and power and place ownership of property, resources, and modes of production in the hands of the government, which would then fairly distribute the wealth back to the masses. According to Marx, the health of society and culture (the actions, values, and beliefs of people at any given time in history) is determined by economic conditions.

In many different historical examples, the *practical* applications of Marxism in both economic and political systems have proven less than successful. Marx's dream of an egalitarian society under state-controlled businesses has, in Russia and many third-world countries, translated into something quite less than egalitarian. Hobbled by bureaucratic constrictions and the inability of state-run organizations to react quickly enough to a global market economy, few Marxist societies around the world have been places where freedom reigned.

If this is true, what does the study of Marxism still have left to offer, particularly to students of literature? As it has been narrowly applied so far, Marxism may not be the alternative solution to problems found in capitalist societies; however, the problems with capitalism that gave rise to Marxism in the nineteenth century still exist. Social and economic conditions continue to shape what we believe and value. As long as the abuses of capitalism—for example: an unfair distribution of wealth and resources; unemployment; and restricted opportunities to education, health care, and economic advancement—exist, a Marxist critique of these conditions is important both to highlighting their existence and to lessening their pervasiveness.

Although Marx viewed history and society primarily through an economic lens, he was also interested in the relationship between economic systems and the production of art. As the first Marxist literary critic, Karl Marx believed that the art produced in any society would somehow reflect and comment upon the basic economic realities in control. A Marxist literary critic believes that a text cannot be separated from the historical moment and cultural situation from which it emerges. Such examinations will necessarily reveal important things about the dominant class, its accompanying ideology, and the effect such circumstances impose upon individuals who must live within such a system. Simply put, Marxist art would ideally embody values of cooperation and equality, while art created in a capitalist system would show signs of decadence and alienation. Since capitalism has remained the dominant economic structure in the Western world, Marxist literary criticism documents the limits of capitalism as it appears in all kinds of Western literature, written across the entire historical spectrum.

Because so much of Edgar Allan Poe's poetry, fiction, and even his essays are deliberately devoid of a definite historical and economic context, a Marxist analysis of his work may initially appear inappropriate or even impossible. Poe was always interested more in the realm of the self-enclosed individual psyche or in the creation of a fantastic world than he was in detailing the social realities of early to mid-nineteenth-century American life. Unlike his literary contemporaries—

transcendentalists such as Henry Thoreau and novelist Herman Melville—Poe did not apply his art directly to the realities of capitalist economics.

All this notwithstanding, a Marxist approach to Poe's work yields interesting insights—albeit well disguised under the perfumed veils of masquerade costumes and highly introverted psychopaths—into the world of nineteenth-century American capitalism. A Marxist reading of Poe might begin with a serious consideration of the level and pervasiveness of violence that take place in his tales of terror and revenge. Surely Poe's portraits of criminal behavior are at least in part a response to the growing violence and arrogance of an increasingly violent and arrogant nineteenth-century America. His male protagonists, as we have seen, are severely isolated individuals with absolutely no connection to the larger community or social fabric.

In *Capital*, Marx referred to capitalists as vampires sucking the life blood out of laborers: "Capital is dead labour which, vampire-like, lives only by sucking living labour, and lives the more, the more labour it sucks" (342). Many of Poe's protagonists resemble the walking undead, drained of purpose, wandering aimlessly through urban streets and cloistered houses searching for someone or something to relive their boredom, to provide a focus to their empty lives. Anonymous men lost in the alleys of anonymous American cities, Poe's urban narrators appear as extreme examples of Marx's alienated factory laborers, the by-products of a vampiric economic system that values profits over people and invests little or nothing in interpersonal relationships and social networks.

While observing the apparently unemployed and definitely discontented urban wanderers in Poe's fiction—the narrators in "The Black Cat," "The Imp of the Perverse," "The Tell-Tale Heart," and "The Man of the Crowd"—a Marxist critic is tempted to explain their perverse obsessional inclinations as the consequence of lives squandered in quiet desperation. Like the industrial working class Marx describes as performing alienated labor that makes them feel mechanical and disempowered at the factory—sentiments that are in turn brought home with them after work—Poe's narrators feel no investment in the betterment of society or themselves. Surrendering rational controls—either through self-indulgence or depreciation of another's life—leads to a chaotic, incomprehensible, but nevertheless passionately felt personal existence. Poe's characters feel most alive when they are engaged in various acts of mayhem and destruction against themselves and others, and a Marxist analysis would surely point out that such a response is not merely an indictment of the individual experiencing it but also the social environment that has produced the individual. Additionally, the intense magnification of the role of the individual in Poe's art—in his separation from the social collective, his rejection of institutions such as law and marriage, and his arrogant notion of self-importance—can be read as a subversive indictment of American individualism. In Poe, as well as in

Marx, the constant and unsatisfying quest to discover some level of meaning under a capitalist system occurs because of the absence of a group identity. Poe's narrators are as much tortured by their awareness of this personal emptiness as they are by attempts to fill the void by destroying other people. In fact, these two impulses actually feed one another.

Although Poe's fiction often resists overt political analysis, a tale such as "Hop-Frog" becomes all the more interesting when interpreted from a Marxist perspective. Although set in a mythical kingdom, because the tale relies so heavily upon inversions of the human-beast and master-slave implications, it invites commentary on the racial institution of slavery that was a contentious issue in the United States during Poe's lifetime. Essentially kidnapped from his "barbarous" homeland, given a new, derisive name and identity by his captors, and forced to remain in the kingdom against his will, Hop-Frog may be racially unspecified but he shares a fate in common with African slaves who likewise "had been carried off from their respective homes" (900) and made to perform for their masters. Other parallels with the institution of slavery are too perva-sive to ignore. The king and his court view Hop-Frog's involuntary servitude as natural, just, and morally uncomplicated, just as those capitalists who bene-fited financially from slavery made similar arguments in its defense. Moreover, the surviving members of the masquerade party are "horror-stricken" by Hop-Frog's "fiery revenge" (908), perhaps unsettled as much by evidence of Hop-Frog's intelligent cunning as they are by his visceral level of revenge. The narrator's closing observation that Hop-Frog and Trippetta "effected their es-cape into their own country" (908) is additional argument for a political read-ing of the fairy tale.

Many of the arguments that suggest a racial interpretation for "Hop-Frog" can also be employed to highlight the relationship between the bourgeoisie and workers under a capitalist society. The story underscores Marx's belief that op-pressed people could only rise up against their oppressors through violent revo-lution. For Marx, freedom is only possible through confrontational struggle; it is a condition that will simply not evolve naturally. In a Marxist reading of this tale, the king and his advisors represent symbolically the capitalist ruling class, while Hop-Frog and Trippetta are the enslaved proletariat. In working to-gether to make their bid for freedom, they follow Marx's prediction that one day the roles of the oppressed and the oppressor will be reversed, and control will ultimately reside with the people rather than the capitalist/king.

Stories such as "The Masque of the Red Death," "The Tell-Tale Heart," and "The Pit and the Pendulum" resemble "Hop-Frog" insofar as they all feature levels of outside tyranny that must be overthrown before the protagonist can be free. While none of these texts confronts the Marxist paradigm of capitalist domination and collective worker struggle explicitly, each nevertheless highlights certain power dynamics that are uniquely illuminated by a Marxist analysis. For example, in "The Masque of the Red Death," Prospero's efforts to avoid the plague can be interpreted as an example of the kind of class domination that parallels the self-interest of the ruling capitalist class. While the common folk are left to deal with the Red Death to the best of their abilities, Prospero safely sequesters himself and his chosen minority behind the protective iron walls of privilege and power. Prospero's guiding sentiment that "the external world could take care of itself" (485) is representative of the same hard-hearted business ethic that Marx associated with an unfettered capitalist economy and its attendant level of social commitment.

Similarly, "The Tell-Tale Heart," read from a Marxist perspective, reveals the story of patriarchal domination and oppression that must be violently confronted. The "vulture eye" of the man in this story, while ambivalent throughout, may thus symbolize the omnipresent "eye" of the bourgeoisie capitalist exerting masterful control over the worker both at home and in the workplace.

The general atmosphere of isolation and expressions of violent discontent that pervade the personal and social worlds of Poe's fiction can be at least partially attributed to the author's own self-perception that in choosing a career in literature (where he also remained critically unappreciated and financially unrewarded) instead of business, he had failed to become one of "America's sons." The early unmitigated scorn of his successful foster father, John Allan, toward Poe's "inappropriate" choice of vocations haunted Poe long after Allan had died. As Charles Baudelaire was first to point out in his 1856 biography, Poe was the quintessential artist figure pressured into psychic and financial distress by the bourgeoisie's quick dismissal of art that was perceived to be neither functional nor marketable. Baudelaire's quasi-Marxist critique insists that although Poe was a writer and not a businessman, he was nonetheless a victim of capitalism's narrow definition of masculine success. Thus, his alienated and socially ostracized fictional protagonists, when read from a Marxist perspective, can be seen to embody sentiments similar to those that Poe himself harbored as he labored within the conforming confines of a capitalist economy and social system.

Since his death, Poe has, of course, become an object of mass consumption by the very culture that once ignored him, a culture whose "mob mentality" was vilified in several of the writer's harshest parodies. All of Poe's fictionalized encounters with the democratic society he simultaneously solicited and scorned suggest that he could often be highly critical of nineteenth-century America. In any event, a Marxist theorist would argue that it is impossible not to read Poe as somehow commenting upon his epoch, even when his work appears most disengaged from American culture. In an age when America's literary and national spirit was shaped by Ralph Waldo Emerson and his belief in self-reliance and an expansionist philosophy, Poe was severely critical of transcendentalism's nebulous metaphysics, democratic spirit, core hopefulness, and trust in the divinity of the self. The transcendentalists found in the individual American a repository of self-reliance and limitless potential; for Poe, this emphasis upon the individual translated into an arrogant superiority that erased all moral prohibitions against even murder and revenge. If the transcendental poet Walt Whitman "sounds [the] barbaric yawp" of capitalism and self- affirmation "over the roofs of the world" (Whitman, 134), Poe must be recognized as the voice from deep within the shadows, an essentially anti-patriotic shriek of pain directed at what is wrong with America.

6

The Origins of the Detective Tale

Think of some of the most famous detectives from literature, the movies, and television: Sherlock Holmes, Sam Spade, Colombo, Philip Marlowe, Perry Mason, Mike Hammer, Dirty Harry, Batman, Spenser, Clarice Starling, Kinsey Millhone, Emma Peel and John Steed, Eliot Ness, Shaft, Jessica "Murder, She Wrote" Fletcher, Scully and Mulder, the detectives in the series *Hill Street Blues* and those who reside at Ed McBain's 87th precinct house. To a greater or lesser extent, all these characters owe their very existence, as well as many of the crime-solving techniques they employ, to the progenitor of the modern detective invented by Edgar Allan Poe, C. Auguste Dupin. Dupin was the first in a long line of literary and celluloid criminal investigators to use careful observation, logical deduction and inference, investigative techniques, imaginative insights, and identification with criminal impulses as central aids to the apprehension of felons.

The Poe protagonists considered so far in this book fall into two general categories: the idealized, dead or dying female, and the first-person male narrator who has either witnessed a supernatural occurrence or has recently participated in a heinous crime. In either case, passive maiden or disturbed sociopath, the universe in which these characters operate is anything but rational. Prematurely buried women rise bloodied and clotted with gore from their sealed crypts, while madmen feel an overwhelming compulsion to reveal criminal acts they have committed in their fury.

In contrast to the perverse and irrational actions that occur in Poe's poetry and tales of murder and suspense, C. Auguste Dupin is a man who strives to place these dark forces under containment. Poe's detectives and criminals are, finally, opposite sides of the same authorial consciousness. The poetical dreamers and hypersensitive protagonists of Poe's fiction generally represent the emotional side of Poe's psyche, while Dupin highlights the intellectual. These two distinct groups of characters suggest the hemispheric specialization of a single brain, as the right hemisphere supports mathematical and reasoned acts of cognition, while more abstract processing, speech, and sounds are processed in the left hemisphere. The core "evil" that fuels Poe's tales of violence is counterpointed in Dupin's efforts to bring justice to play upon criminal endeavors. Dupin represents the balancing authority against the principles of violence and mayhem found throughout Poe's fictional universe.

In Poe's horror tales, the sensational nature of murder and its aftermath give rise to individual energies that always threaten to verge out of control. Regardless of how careful the murdering protagonist has been in the commission of his particular crime, passion usually overwhelms intellect. Dupin, on the other hand, is both inquisitive and highly focused. He never credits irrational or insane acts, choosing instead to conduct his life according to a master plan that is guided by reason and a highly developed intuitive sense. Although Dupin enters into situations that are charged with emotions and confusion—as everything becomes a potential clue, all of life becomes animated with potential significance—the detective maintains his cool. Completely self-contained and deigning to enter the social sphere only to exhibit his crime-solving genius to the embarrassment of the authorities, the great detective operates on a plane of his own making, securely confident that he possesses the rational skills necessary to reestablishing order. Thus in the tales of terror and suspense, Poe's protagonists relinquish whatever remains of their self-discipline and rational faculties. In the detective tales, however, it is the discipline of logic and reason that sustains the narrative. Dupin exhibits the sharpest mental faculties—the rational powers that Poe himself called *ratiocination*—that permit him to stay in control of himself and the situation. The operative word in the detective tale is balance: Dupin employs the attributes of ratiocination to maintain a fixed level of control amid the chaos of a violent and bloody moment.

The three Poe texts that revolve around Dupin feature a super-sleuth who is the dominant presence in each of the tales in which he appears. The eventual solution to solving crimes that have baffled the police as well as the nameless narrator who accompanies Dupin is never doubted, at least by Dupin himself. To solve insoluble crimes, Dupin's mind employs the imagination of the poet and the analytic intelligence of the mathematician. He entertains a perfect balance of analysis and speculative insight rendered all the more effective by his close identification with the criminal and his thought processes. For Dupin, solving a crime is not a moral act performed for the betterment of society or for the self-improvement of the criminal but, rather, an intellectual and intuitive exercise, perhaps best aligned to Poe's own lifelong fascination with puzzles and cryptograms.

Return, for a moment, to the list of detectives that begins this chapter. In spite of their similar occupations, these characters are unique individuals. Surely the highly intelligent and athletic Mrs. Emma Peel (the female detective from the 1960s television show *The Avengers*), her fierce commitment to thwarting British terrorism softened only by her feminine demeanor and attire, is far removed from the hard-boiled, hard-drinking masculine tradition that would include Mike Hammer and Philip Marlowe. Such differences notwithstanding, all these detectives share important similarities. Perhaps the first thing to notice is how often these same characters reappear in different episodes and original novels. One distinguishing element of the detective tradition born through the character of Poe's Dupin is that the detective neither dies nor disappears; he or she must return to scenes of new crimes not only to sustain and enrich their own professional legacies but also to underscore the point that the tradition of the detective genre is largely about stability and control. Thus, the prefect of police solicits Dupin's assistance in "The Mystery of Marie Roget" because of his success in solving the earlier criminal case in "The Murders in the Rue Morgue." Each time one of these famous investigators makes a reappearance, it essentially underscores a core element of the genre itself: that order will eventually prevail over even the most difficult of circumstances and that the criminal will be punished in some appropriate way. After all, how many narratives featuring any of these aforementioned detectives ever end with an unsolved case or with the criminal escaping triumphantly?

The plethora of modern detectives who follow Dupin strive to attain his level of perfectibility and genius. Many of them operate in a realm that pits them in direct competition with the police, and usually by the end of the investigation, most modern detectives—like Dupin himself—end up solving the case without much assistance from the police. Although professionally successful and always intelligent, twentieth-century sleuths are frequently dependent upon their athleticism, street wits and fists, skill in the martial arts, or the use of weaponry while Dupin relies solely upon his cerebral superiority. But modern detectives also rely upon Dupin's logical capabilities as an aid to solving crimes. Scully and Mulder spend vast amounts of time and energy in each episode of *The X-Files* tracking leads, dissecting evidence, interviewing witnesses, and assembling data. All of this is especially important for their particular types of investigations, as they must frequently prove that supernatural phenomena are real, that the speculative realm can be logically proven. In Thomas Harris's novel *The Silence of the Lambs*, Clarice Starling relies on both feminine intuition and logical deduction to solve the case of Buffalo Bill, the serial killer who is constructing a "female suit" out of the skins of his dead victims. Like Dupin, Starling is a detective who learns the skill of disciplining herself in the face of intense levels of violence and chaos. She studies the details of the case and logically reasons that there is a sewing connection between the killer and his first victim, Fredrica Bimmel. Through the course of the novel, Starling plays cat-and-mouse games with both Buffalo Bill and the cannibal-psychiatrist, Hannibal Lecter, that closely resemble the highly competitive relationship that plays out between Dupin and the Minister D in "The Purloined Letter." In both Harris's novel and Poe's story, the detective must outwit the criminal intellectually, garnering information and using it against him. In both plots, evil is overcome by detectives who place themselves in opposition to the destruction and mayhem that are the consequences of criminal behavior. Dupin and Starling would restore a measure of the individuality and dignity stolen from the victims in each respective text.

THE MURDERS IN THE RUE MORGUE (1841)

Although this long short story was first published in *Graham's Magazine* for April 1841, Poe may have arrived at the idea for this tale as early as 1838, when *Burton's Gentleman's Magazine* serialized an article on the "Unpublished Passages in the Life of Vidocq, the French Minister of Police." Poe, an avid reader of urban crime histories and reports, read the entire series. He may also have read an article in the *Shrewsbury Chronicle* for July 1834 that described how a gang of professional criminals had taught a baboon to commit burglaries by climbing into the windows of upper-level apartments. Additional inspiration undoubtedly occurred in 1839 when an orangutan (ourang-outang) was publicly exhibited for August and September at the Masonic Hall in Philadelphia while Poe resided in the city. A first French translation of Poe's tale (without any acknowledgment of Poe's authorship) appeared in *La Quotidienne*, June 11–13, 1846.

SETTING AND PLOT

In reading the "Unpublished Passages in the Life of Vidocq, the French Minister of Police," Poe may well have decided upon the setting for "The Murders in the Rue Morgue" as well as a prototype for his own detective. Poe's tale takes place in the heart of urban Paris in the mid-nineteenth century. The sense of a bustling street life and of buildings pressed closely to the sidewalks where people pass in a continuous stream is a notable feature of this tale.

"Murders" begins with a general discourse on the satisfaction the analytical mind obtains in those activities that call into play the ability to "disentangle" a problem. By this, Poe refers to the sense of success that attends the solving "of enigmas, of conundrums, of hieroglyphics; exhibiting in his solutions of each a degree of *acumen* which appears to the ordinary apprehension praeternatural" (397). In other words, some minds work better than others at solving complicated problems. This will be important later in the story in explaining why Dupin succeeds in analyzing the crime scene while others, specifically the police and the narrator, do not. Dupin's mental faculties are simply superior. In keeping with this discourse, the narrator posits that the game of draughts, or checkers, is a greater gauge of analytical ability than chess because in checkers a player must always be aware of things *external* to the game itself: the facial expressions of an opponent, the words spoken in conversation during the course of the game that reveal his opponent's intentions. For the narrator, checkers allows the mind to employ the fullest range of its analytic resources: "While the analyst is necessarily ingenious, the ingenious man is often remarkably incapable of analysis" (399).

This rather long discussion of board games and the narrator's opinion on cognitive thinking is a prelude to his introduction of Monsieur C. Auguste Dupin. A native of Paris, Dupin is young, comes from an aristocratic family, but has been "reduced to such poverty that the energy of his character succumbed beneath it, and he ceased to bestir himself in the world, or to care for the retrieval of his fortunes" (400). Dupin retains enough money to live as a retired recluse, and he and the narrator, who share an apartment, spend their days reading books in complete seclusion without friends or visitors. Only at night do the two emerge "into the streets, arm in arm, continuing the topics of the day or roaming far and wide until a late hour, seeking, amid the wild lights and shadows of the populous city, that infinity of mental excitement which quiet observation can afford" (401).

One night, while reading the local paper, the two men become interested in the murder of two women, Madame L'Espanaye and her daughter, Camille. Living in a fourth-floor apartment, the two women were brutally murdered: the daughter's corpse inserted up a chimney, feet first, while the mother's head was nearly severed from her body. Their apartment was found "in the wildest disorder" (405), but there was apparently neither a forced entry—all the windows were closed and nailed shut and the door was locked from the inside—nor a motive for robbery, as upon the floor "two bags, containing nearly four thousand francs in gold" (405) were recovered. Several people claim to have heard the voice "of a foreigner" (407) from inside the apartment, but since there were no actual eyewitnesses to the crime, the police are baffled.

Dupin, who knows the prefect of police, gets permission to investigate the crime scene. While the narrator "could merely agree with all of Paris in considering [the deaths] an insoluble mystery" (411), Dupin shocks his friend by announcing that he has already solved the case and expects the arrival at any moment of a person implicated in the crimes. While they await this person, Dupin elaborates upon his discovery. Dupin began his investigation with a thorough consideration of the surrounding neighborhood as well as the L'Espanaye apartment. His careful scrutiny revealed that one of the nails supposedly locking the windows had broken and that this was the means of entry and exit for the murderer. His inspection of the neighborhood taught him that only someone with superhuman strength could manage to climb four stories into the apartment and "thrust the body *up* such an aperture so forcibly that the united vigor of several persons was found barely sufficient to drag it *down!*" (422). Dupin then shows the narrator a notice he has published in the newspaper claiming that he has captured an escaped Ourang-Outang and is awaiting its owner to come and claim it.

A short time later, a sailor arrives at Dupin's door to claim the animal. Confronted with Dupin's knowledge of the crime, the sailor tells the story of how he had captured the animal in Borneo and brought it to Paris where it then escaped its cage with the sailor's razor in hand. The sailor followed the ape to the L'Espanaye apartment where he witnessed the murders from a perch at the top of a lightning rod. After watching the carnage take place, he "hurried at once home—dreading the consequences of the butchery, and gladly abandoning, in his terror, all solicitude about the fate of the Ourang-Outang" (430).

CHARACTERS

The narrator plays the part of the straight man in this tale. His role is very different from most of the first-person storytellers in Poe, as he is essentially an observer whose sole purpose is to offer fumbling assistance to Dupin—usually by way of inaccurate observations, suppositions, and conclusions that the detective then corrects. It is immediately clear that detective writer Arthur Conan Doyle modeled his own lovable and ineffectual character, Watson, directly after Poe's narrator. He stands in awe of Dupin, not only as a friend, but more because the latter is in possession of such acute mental faculties and lives a life of eccentric proportions.

C. Auguste Dupin's entrance into the world must be heralded as one of the great literary achievements of all time, and "The Murders in the Rue Morgue" as the beginning of modern detective fiction. What is perhaps most impressive about Dupin's character, however, is not merely that he is capable of solving difficult crimes but the manner in which he does so. In addition to relying upon the facts of careful observation and logical analysis, Dupin possesses "the wild fervor, and the vivid freshness of imagination" (400). He lives an eccentric life, more akin to a vampire in his nocturnal wanderings than to the traditional policeman. But it is Dupin's essential "strangeness," his deviation from the mundane in both personal behavior and approach to criminology, that makes him such an inventive criminologist as well as an interesting character to the narrator and the reader alike. Moreover, the police remain confused by the Rue Morgue murders because the crimes make no sense: robbery was not a motive and the singular level of brutality performed against the defenseless women goes beyond any rational explanation. Dupin, however, is able to supersede such restrictive thinking because in addition to studying the facts of the case, his deep personal connection to the exotic and peculiar permit him to conceive of things in ways that others cannot.

Dupin is part logician, part Romantic poet, and part metaphysician, but his supreme crime-solving gift is his imagination, which gives him particular insight into the realm of the irrational, criminal mind. Since no witness agrees with any other on the language spoken by the murderer, Dupin quickly eliminates the possibility that the crime was committed by a human being. On the other hand, Dupin's rational powers do not allow him (in contrast to so many of the characters from Poe's horror tales) to consider supernatural explanations: "Madame and Mademoiselle L'Espanaye were not destroyed by spirits. The doers of the deed were material, and escaped materially" (417). Dupin merely operates on the theory that the extraordinary always manifests itself in the ordinary. While such abilities to deviate from the normal do not extend into the paranormal, they do serve to stimulate Dupin's imaginative capabilities and enable him to conceptualize a crime that has never before occurred: "It is by these deviations from the plane of the ordinary, that reason feels its way, if at all, in its search for the true. In investigations such as we are now pursuing, it should not be so much asked 'what has occurred,' as 'what has occurred that has never occurred before' " (414).

The prefect of police occupies only a small role in this tale, that of foil to Dupin's genius. When Dupin solves the case, the prefect is both envious and further baffled. He probably only allowed Dupin access to the crime scene because the prefect was convinced that Dupin could not solve the case and because the prefect was desperate for help. The prefect's investigative abilities are too narrow because the police are unable to think beyond the details and facts supplied by the evidence. Dupin dismisses such an approach because, like most rationalists devoid of speculative insights, the policeman "impaired his vision by holding the object too close. He might see, perhaps, one or two points with unusual clearness, but in so doing he, necessarily, lost sight of the matter as a whole" (412).

THEMES

The detective story became an especially important genre for expressing Poe's unique talents and interests. It supplied him the opportunity to explore further his attraction to logic and analysis, so clearly evident in the formulation of his literary essays and the cryptic tale "The Gold Bug." But in his hands the genre was also broad enough to continue to explore the realm of the unfettered imagination, both in terms of how Dupin employed his imagination to solve crimes and in the particularly bizarre—and original—nature of crime itself, "the *outre* character of its features" (414). The detective, for Poe, was a kind of literary critic who must read and analyze the themes and situations in which he finds himself, interpreting the patterns and symbols that the criminal, who occupies a role that simulates that of the creative artist, leaves behind. Poe himself was profoundly aware of these parallels, as he indicated in a 1846 letter: "In the 'Murders in the Rue Morgue,' for instance, there is the ingenuity of unravelling a web which you yourself (the author) have woven for the express purpose of unravelling" (Ostrom, 328). The theme of this story—and, for that matter, all of Poe's detective tales—is that the entire narrative is itself a puzzle that must be solved, a pattern that must be deciphered. A series of links or clues are brought into juxtaposition with one another and from this an associative process begins to take shape. Thus, in "Murders in the Rue Morgue," the strange language used by the murderer that no one in the apartment building understands is linked to the broken nail in the fourth-floor window, which, in turn, is connected to the fact that the unique brutality of the L'Espanaye murders appears to be motiveless. All of this points the way for Dupin to reach his conclusion that the killer was not human. In Poe, the detective story relies upon logic and reason, but only as a means to an end that underscores the extreme absurdities of life, the extraordinary nature of reality itself. The closer Poe's tales of ratiocination are examined, the more they reveal the full range of their author's talent in the merging of his various oppositional interests.

THE MYSTERY OF MARIE ROGET (1841)

This is the second of the Dupin detective tales, first serialized in three parts in *Snowden's Ladies Companion* beginning in November 1842, continuing in the December 1842 number, and concluding in the February 1843 issue. This long tale should probably be classified as a novella rather than a short story.

SETTING AND PLOT

"The Mystery of Marie Roget" is subtitled "A Sequel to 'Murders in the Rue Morgue,' " because it continues to embellish the history of Dupin, the now famous Parisian detective. "Marie Roget" is actually based upon the real (and unsolved) murder case of Mary Cecilla Rogers, who was kidnapped from a New York City cigar store where she worked. Her corpse was found in the Hudson River on July 28, 1841. Poe transported the story's setting from New York to Paris in order to bring the crime directly to Dupin. Thus in Poe's fictionalization of the crime, the American locales associated with Rogers's murder became French: the tobacco shop turned into a perfume shop; Weehawken, New Jersey, the last place where Rogers was seen alive, became the Barriere du Roule; the Hudson River reappeared as the Seine; and, of course, Rogers's name is given a French twist, changed to Marie Roget.

Dupin is called into the investigation because of his success in solving the murders in the Rue Morgue. Once again, the prefect of police is confounded by a brutal killing. On this occasion, a beautiful young girl disappeared mysteriously from work and her mother's home, only to turn up four days later as a corpse floating in the Seine. On the shore, Marie's gloves and a monogrammed handkerchief bearing her name were found. The brush around the site indicated signs of struggle. Rope marks found on her wrists and abrasions around her neck and waist suggested that she was pulled some distance by a rope. It appeared as if she had been gagged by a strip of her own petticoat, and the cause of death was either strangulation or suffocation. "The general impression, so far as we were enabled to glean it from the newspapers, seemed to be, that Marie had been the victim of a *gang* of desperados—that by these she had been borne across the river, maltreated, and murdered" (517).

As the narrator reads to Dupin the sensationalized details of the crime and the inane analyses of it published in the daily Parisian papers, the detective finds reason to dismiss all their credibility and explanations. For example, the papers report that Marie was observed in the company of a sailor during the week of her disappearance. While the journalists and police do not know what to make of this occurrence, the detective speculates that there must be a connection between this sailor and the murder, especially since Marie Roget was engaged to be married to another man. Dupin concludes that the articles of clothing left along the side of the Seine and the signs of a struggle nearby were all planted by the murderer to make it appear as though Marie had been victimized by a gang of men. Dupin posits that the murder was actually committed by a single individual. A gang, Dupin reasons, would not have allowed all this evidence to be left behind for the police to find. Only an individual, "his fears redoubled within him . . . and fleeing from the wrath to come" (546), would be paralyzed sufficiently to disregard the items of Marie Roget's clothing. Furthermore, the crime site showed "evident traces of some heavy burden having been dragged along it" (547). Several males would have simply lifted Marie; only an individual would have been forced to drag her. That is why her body was found with rope abrasions around her wrists and a cloth belt fashioned around her waist—to help the murderer pull her body.

Dupin concludes that Marie Roget's death came at the hands of a secret lover, the sailor with whom she was last seen, who dumped her body from a boat, and then set the boat adrift on the Seine to confuse the police. The story ends not in the apprehension of the murderous sailor, but with Dupin's insistence that if the authorities can track down the boat the sailor used to ferry Marie's body out into the river, they will be able to trace it back to the sailor: "This boat shall guide us, with a rapidity which will surprise even ourselves, to him who employed it in the midnight of the fatal Sabbath" (552).

CHARACTERS

As in "Murders in the Rue Morgue," the narrator's role is primarily to serve as Dupin's assistant. He provides information, mostly gleaned from newspaper accounts dealing with the murder, to which Dupin then reacts. In a way, the narrator is a stimulus for the detective's intellect. At various points throughout Poe's detective tales the narrator almost "disappears" from the narrative, even though events and Dupin's speech are always filtered through his consciousness.

Dupin's role as a detective in "Marie Roget" differs substantially from his highly active involvement in "Murders in the Rue Morgue" and "The Purloined Letter." In "Murders" and "Letter," he must actually visit the crime scenes, observe and record information relevant to solving the respective crimes, and in "The Purloined Letter" he becomes the sole agent for obtaining the stolen property. In "Marie Roget," Dupin never leaves his library.

These differences notwithstanding, Dupin's character as super-intelligent criminologist and acute psychologist of the human personality is still very evident in "Marie Roget." Applying the same mental principles that enabled him to solve the double homicide in "Murders," Dupin reconstructs the murderer's frame of mind and pieces together the facts of this "ordinary, although an atrocious, instance of crime" (519). Many of Dupin's suppositions emerge as a direct response to the various Parisian newspaper accounts of the murder. The detective disagrees with nearly every article the narrator shares with him. Dupin understands that the newspapers have simply amassed details; they have failed to uncover a methodology for comprehending those details, a criminal design that allows these details to make sense. Armed with his intuitive skills, he takes what he needs from information and clues distributed in the Paris newspapers to discern certain criminal patterns that the journalists, like the police, are incapable of recognizing. For example, because of the cloth around Marie's waist, the detective concludes that she was not murdered by a group of men as the papers suggest, but by a single slayer who fashioned this belt in order to drag his victim to the river.

THEMES

"Marie Roget," like Poe's other Dupin-centered tales, focuses its central theme on the brilliance of the detective. Despite Dupin's brilliance, however, his role in this story appears weaker, perhaps because unlike his work in "Murders" and "The Purloined Letter," the detective remains removed from the narrative action of solving the crime itself. Critics tend to agree that this is the least satisfying of the three Dupin tales. Some have speculated this is so because Poe based the story upon a real-life murder that he himself was trying to solve.

Although "Marie Roget" concludes with a certain lack of closure—the criminal remains at large and Dupin never does interact with him—it is still a narrative that relies heavily upon the theme of a superior analytical ability that reconstructs the crime accurately in spite of conflicting evidence and false clues. Even as the Paris newspapers inflame public opinion with their various (and erroneous) speculations about the crime and its perpetrator, Dupin keeps his rational wits about him throughout. Remaining immune to public opinion and the details of sensationalistic brutality that distinguish this case, Dupin offers himself as a model of the self-disciplined and self-contained detective—the prototype for future criminal investigators from Sherlock Holmes to Colombo.

THE PIT AND THE PENDULUM (1843)

One of the great horror stories of the world, this tale was first published in *The Gift: A Christmas and New Year's Present,* MDCCCXLIII (1843) and revised for publication in the *Broadway Journal* of May 17, 1845.

SETTING AND PLOT

The narrative begins with "the dread sentence of death" (491), the last words the narrator hears before fainting. What follows is a series of gruesome tortures that befall the speaker of the tale as he struggles against the sadistic inventions imposed upon him by a Spanish Inquisitional tribunal that has condemned him to death. The setting of the entire tale is vintage Poe: a one-room cell, apparently made of iron plate walls, that is capable of changing shape—from a square to a lozenge. In the center of the cell is a deep, circular pit that descends many feet into water. The narrator discovers the dimensions of this torture chamber by degrees, for at first he awakens into total blackness, "the blackness of eternal night" (492).

— 113 —

In part to calm "the tumultuous motion of the heart" (493), the narrator explores his dungeon "to deduce my real condition" (494). The atmosphere of the dungeon "was intolerably close" (493). While carefully measuring the perimeter of his cell in order to determine the shape and size of the chamber, the narrator slips and discovers the pit directly in front of him. Another step, and he would have fallen to his death.

Thirsty, hungry, exhausted, and highly agitated, the narrator drinks from a drugged pitcher of water. He falls asleep, and awakens to find himself strapped to a wooden platform in the center of the cell. The room is no longer in darkness, so the narrator notices a painted figure of Father Time on the ceiling above him. The figure is holding a huge pendulum that bears a razor-sharp edge. This scythe not only moves diagonally, but also descends, and it is designed to "cross the region of the heart" (500). The pendulum moves ever so slowly in its descent, and the narrator realizes suddenly that his tormentors have brought light into the cell so that their victim will be able to watch his own slow death.

Taking up a piece of meat still within his reach, the condemned man rubs it across the bandages that secure him to the platform. Hundreds of rats that share the cell with him swarm forward and begin gnawing at the bonds. "Plainly I perceived the loosening of the bandage. I knew that in more than one place it must be already severed. With a more than human resolution I lay *still*" (503). As the descending blade begins to sever his flesh, the straps part and he slithers free.

As soon as he escapes, the pendulum is withdrawn into the ceiling. The walls of the prison grow suddenly hot to the touch and begin to change shape, pulling together, squeezing the narrator ever closer toward the pit as the faces of the painted figures take on a terrifying form. Just as he is about to topple over, the walls pull back, and the narrator is miraculously saved by the invading French army.

CHARACTERS

Condemned for an unknown crime, by an unknown group of Inquisitors in Toledo, the anonymous narrator is the focus of all the human action in this tale. In short, we know nothing about this prisoner—he had no past history, and his future appears very much in doubt. Except for the salvational figure of General Lasalle, no characters in the story are named. The protagonist's task is simply to save himself. Around him are the nefarious devices of the Inquisition: the transforming dungeon, a razor-edged pendulum, the ghastly figures of the tribunal painted upon the walls, a pit that is an entrance to hell. The narrator is surrounded by shadows cast by other people, but only the physical tools of his torment are ever clearly visible. His isolation is as deep and as terrifying as the blackness of the pit itself. His only communication with another living organism is with the rats, who disgust him at the same time that they save his life. Such a horrific environment forces the narrator into a battle that is as much centered inside his own head as it is in the excruciating tortures designed by his jailers. Although he is always on the verge of screaming hysterically, fading in and out of consciousness, the narrator's desperate efforts to prolong his life are linked inextricably to the manner in which he conducts himself.

THEMES

At first glance, the reader may find it odd that an analysis of "The Pit and the Pendulum" is included in this chapter dealing with Poe's detective fiction. But the tale's inclusion is no accident, especially as it was written about the same time that Poe composed the Dupin narratives. Even more important, the theme of this story parallels those found in the detective tales: the ability of the rational mind to assert itself over irrational circumstances. Indeed, "The Pit and the Pendulum" has been read by critic David Hirsch as the ultimate existential allegory of an anguished soul confronted by the blackness of existence in an absurd universe whose shape and meaning can never be ascertained. Yet, just as Dupin uses logic and cool analysis to exert control over the brutality and madness that produces the murders of innocent women, the narrator in "The Pit and the Pendulum" must endeavor to reason his way out of personal fear and despair. Against the "frantic madness" and "the sweep of the fearful scimitar" (500), the narrator struggles not to panic. "For the first time during many hours—or perhaps days—I *thought*" (501). His powers of reason rise up against "the nervous energy of despair" (502).

Madness presses in upon him throughout the story; each inventive torture pushes him closer to the pit, which symbolizes the abandonment of reason, the "hole" in logic. "Long suffering had nearly annihilated all my ordinary powers of mind" (500). Yet the narrator, like a good detective, reasons his way out of each horrific situation. It is his powers of rational thought that provide "a more than human resolution [to] lay *still*" (503) while rats "swarmed upon me in ever accumulating heaps" (503). From ascertaining the dimensions of his cell amid total blackness to figuring out a method of self-extrication from underneath the pendulum's blade, the narrator saves himself not only from physical death but also from a death of his mind (the latter may be the real goal of the Inquisition's devious tortures). As Dupin's ratiocinative attributes produce a clarity of vision that reigns over the criminal's efforts to foment chaos, the theme of "The Pit and the Pendulum" also centers upon the virtues of self-discipline and self-control. The narrator's consciousness and imagination are under constant assault by this nightmarish situation. But his intellect remains intact through-out, and he ultimately survives because his rational faculties buy him time to be rescued. In spite of ample opportunity to do so, he neither succumbs to the traps of the Inquisition nor to the horrors of his own imagination.

THE PURLOINED LETTER (1844)

The third tale in the Dupin detective trilogy, the story was first published in the annual *The Gift: A Christmas, New Year, and Birthday Present, MDCCCXLV* (actually published in September 1844). An abridgement appeared in *Chamber's Edinburgh Journal* for November 30, 1844.

SETTING AND PLOT

The narrator and Dupin are at home in their apartment located in the center of Paris on an autumn evening just after dusk. Their relaxing evening of smoking pipes and enjoying the presence of each other's company is interrupted by a visit from the prefect of police. He is welcomed by the two inhabitants of the apartment "for there was nearly half as much of the entertaining as of the contemptible about the man, and we had not seen him for years" (680). The prefect explains the reason for his visit. There is a case that is confusing him. At first, the policeman is cryptic in his description of the specifics involved, but Dupin soon gets more information. The case is "an affair demanding the greatest secrecy" (681) because it involves the "honor of a personage of most exalted station" (682). Dupin and the narrator learn that a letter has been stolen from the bedroom of a socially prominent woman who has been having an illicit affair with one of her husband's associates. Since this woman is closely aligned with men of power in the French government, the man who purloined it, the Minister D, intends to use it as an object for blackmailing this woman for political advantage. The prefect's problem is regaining the letter discreetly. Since the woman is offering a "prodigious" (686) reward for the letter's return, the prefect suggests that Dupin and he should share the money if Dupin can somehow retrieve the letter.

The prefect explains that he and his men already made a "thorough search of the Minister's hotel . . . [despite] the danger which would result from giving him reason to suspect our design" (683). They have examined the Minister D's room for secret drawers, even the chairs and tables have been overturned and carefully analyzed for the possibility of hollow legs and arms. "We scrutinized each individual square inch throughout the premises, including the two houses immediately adjoining, with the microscope" (685).

A month or so later, the policeman returns to the apartment belonging to Dupin and the narrator. The detective instructs the prefect to issue a check for fifty thousand francs, and after he does so, Dupin gives him the purloined letter. The prefect "appeared absolutely thunder-stricken" (688), but does not stop to inquire how Dupin obtained the letter, presumably because he is in a mad rush to deliver it back to its rightful owner. After he leaves, Dupin explains to the narrator that it took him only two trips to Minister D's apartment to both uncover and retrieve the letter that the police could not recover in a week's exhaustive search. Dupin knew that the police had conducted a thorough investigation, and "had the letter been deposited within the range of their search, these fellows would, beyond a question, have found it" (688).

Dupin's method of retrieving the letter was to identify with Minister D's unique personality. Most men would "proceed to conceal a letter . . . at least in some out-of-the-way hole or corner" (610), and the police just assumed that the minister would do the same. But Dupin took into consideration the Minister D's individuality; he knew that the minister was "both a mathematician and a poet, and my measures were adapted to his capacity" (693). The minister's cunning intellect afforded him the ability to anticipate that the police would conduct just such a search of his dwelling and possessions, so he simply chose to leave the letter unconcealed in a card rack among his other papers. In this way, it was completely overlooked by the police, but "so *very* self-evident" (694) to Dupin that the detective finds it with little effort.

Dupin entraps Minister D by pretending to forget his gold snuffbox upon the table. The next day when he returns for it, he brings along a facsimile of the letter in question. Arranging beforehand for a gun to be discharged in the street directly below, Dupin uses the distraction to exchange the letters when Minister D is drawn to the window because of the loud noise. Dupin elected to switch the letters rather than to steal it outright because he feared that its loss would be noticed and, more important, because he wanted the minister to operate as if he still owned it: "Thus will he inevitably commit himself, at once, to his political destruction" (697).

CHARACTERS

As in the other Dupin stories, the narrator's role is primarily that of a listener and recorder (for the reader) of the events that take place. Occasionally he asks a question of the detective, but mostly he is an observer present at the two meetings that take place between Dupin and the prefect. For the second half of the story, his job is to listen to the strategy that Dupin employed to recapture the missing letter.

In "The Murders in the Rue Morgue" and "The Mystery of Marie Roget," the prefect of police assumes only a cursory function: he provides Dupin with the facts of each case that are necessary for the detective to solve it. But in "The Purloined Letter," the prefect is present for nearly half the tale, and during this time he occupies the center of the narrative. His role, however, remains the same in all three of Poe's detective tales: he is a simple man who can offer only simple solutions to complex situations. His core defect as a criminal investigator remains his inability to step back from close attention to details and allow the nature of the crime to reveal its own inimitable pattern. Although he certainly respects Dupin's skills, the reader senses that he does not particularly like the detective; his gibes about Dupin's "odd notions" (680) reflect more a jealous contempt than a friendly recognition of eccentric differences. Perhaps the prefect includes Dupin in these criminal investigations in the secret hope that he will fail. If Dupin were not to succeed in cracking a crime that has the police baffled, then that would, by implication, place the prefect on the same intellectual level as Dupin. In the case of the purloined letter, Dupin's recovery of the stolen correspondence stupefies the policeman, but it also rewards him financially. Moreover, as the prefect will be the sole person to explain to the powerful socialite how her letter was obtained, Dupin's efforts may potentially end up enhancing the prefect's reputation as a criminal investigator, as he is now in a position to assume full credit for its recovery.

Dupin's abilities to pay close attention to the particulars of a criminal case are what distinguish him from the police, who are mired in theories of motivation, assumptions based upon previous investigative experience, and general patterns of criminal behavior. As in "Murders in the Rue Morgue," Dupin solves this case by looking for the extraordinary to manifest itself in the ordinary, by paying attention to details easily overlooked, and by stressing the value of the seemingly irrelevant. To hide the letter in plain sight, after all, is to make the ordinary into the extraordinary.

"The Purloined Letter," however, far more than the other two stories in which he appears, stresses Dupin's ability to identify with his opponent, to enter into the criminal psyche. According to critic Leroy Lad Panek, one of Poe's major contributions to the creation of the detective story was the design of a worthy antagonist for Dupin; their competition gives this tale its dramatic energy (30). Indeed, the intellects of both men, Dupin and Minister D, are identified in many ways. Even the choice of the letter "D" to begin the minister's last name is meant to suggest his close connection—perhaps "doubling" is even more accurate—to Dupin. When the prefect of police says that the minister is "only one remove from a fool," being a poet, Dupin confesses, "I have been guilty of a certain doggerel myself" (684). The careful reader recognizes immediately that what the prefect dismisses as a fool, Dupin appreciates as an intuitive part of himself. Like Poe, who was also a poet, Dupin understands that while poetry itself is not typically associated with crime solving, the poet's powers of intuition, inclusive observation, and imaginative capacities make him a worthy adversary for any criminal mind. The Minister D has far more in common with Dupin than he does with the prefect, for had the minister only been logical and mathematical, he would have been captured by the equally analytical prefect. But because the minister possesses also the poetic imagination scorned by the prefect, he rises above the level of police intelligence and enters into the sphere where Dupin resides. This is why only Dupin is capable of capturing him, because they coexist on a similar plane. The individual most capable of solving the mysteries of crime is an individual who possesses insight into the mysteries of human nature, as well as science and logic.

Unlike "The Murders in the Rue Morgue," which relies heavily upon Dupin's use of logic to create an associative web that links together the separate pieces of evidence, "The Purloined Letter" features Dupin's poetical attributes. Poe subscribed to the romantic maxim that intuitive inspiration was superior to analytical reason, and "The Purloined Letter" is one of his most persuasive arguments for this position. It is because he possesses the observational skills of a poet that the detective notices a letter that is noticeably different—that is, crumpled and dirty—from the usual methodical habits of Minister D. Where common and easily discarded objects are overlooked by the police in their search for a clever hiding place, Dupin the poetic investigator is apt to pay attention to what others cannot see, to find significance in the mundane, which is, incidentally, also the goal of any poet serious about his craft.

Poe offers us in Dupin a detective seemingly unburdened by his own "heart of darkness," who maintains as clean a separation between himself and his role as a detective as he does from the police whose collective efforts he both scorns and transcends. For Dupin, detection is merely a game, akin to playing checkers, filling in a crossword puzzle, or solving a mathematical equation. Once the case is solved, he loses interest in it and in the job of being a detective, presumably returning to his quiet world of books and daily conversation with the unnamed narrator; his identity is not wedded to his work. Many of the contemporary detectives who have since inherited Dupin's job, in contrast, find it impossible to separate their personalities from their occupation. Detectives such as Philip Marlowe, Spenser, Mike Hammer, and even Batman labor in a harsher and bleaker atmosphere where it is often difficult to distinguish the detective from the criminal, the good man from the madman. For many of these latter-day investigators, solving criminal cases is their vital last link to a common humanity.

THEMES

"The Purloined Letter" is arguably the most famous and popular of Poe's detective tales. It definitely is the most precise of the three in its narrative design and execution. In his essay "The Philosophy of Composition," Poe insisted that a successful work of art must contain nothing superfluous to the plot; that is, its themes must "proceed, step by step, to its completion with the precision and rigid consequence of a mathematical problem" (1375). These elements of precision and concision are what distinguish "The Purloined Letter," as it maintains a perfect sense of balance between its simplicity of design and its increasing sense of desperate urgency to recover the lost letter. Dupin enjoys the challenge of, and solution to, the problem. His gratification is akin to what a student of mathematics feels in arriving at the answer to a vexing equation—a mixture of intellectual and emotional satisfaction.

Although the narrative is told "backwards"—the action essentially over before the tale is complete—this effect also contributes to the overall structure of the detective story, for this method of narration places Dupin completely at the center of events. Dupin's explanation of his investigation procedure is described almost as a series of recollections; at home with pipe in hand, sitting in his comfortable library, he elaborates upon the theme of the story: his method of analysis. The tale itself may be narrated through another person, but no one is in a position to contradict or to interrupt Dupin. Even Poe's first-person narrators in the horror tales are interrupted by the police or the voice of their own consciences. The detective, however, remains at the center of the action—how he defines the problem and its solution is the thematic crux of the story.

This technique of telling the story backwards through a series of recollections or flashbacks is another aspect of Poe that has influenced other detectives and detective fiction that followed Dupin. Many Hollywood detective films rely upon a narrative voice that comments upon action that has taken place in the past—for example, "The blonde's high heels announced her arrival before she entered my office to tell me her problem." Through his narrator, Watson, Arthur Conan Doyle often employs a similar method of narration, explaining the investigative procedures of his detective, Sherlock Holmes, after the case has already been solved. This narrative strategy emphasizes that the actual events of the detective story are less important than the manner in which the detective assembles them into a comprehensible understanding.

Additionally, Dupin feels an even greater sense of accomplishment in the thwarting of Minister D because "at Vienna once, [he] did me an evil turn, which I told him, quite good-humoredly, that I should remember" (698). The tale, then, can also be read as a theme of revenge and poetic justice (the facsimile letter that Dupin leaves for the minister to find contains a mocking citation in French from Crebillon's revenge play *Atree*). Like another skilled and dispassionate revenger, Montressor in "The Cask of Amontillado," Dupin obtains a particular satisfaction in the outwitting of his unsuspecting victim.

ALTERNATE READING: PSYCHOANALYTICAL CRITICISM

The preceding chapter's "Alternate Reading" section considered Poe's work from a Marxist perspective. This chapter will examine Poe in light of arguably the other most important intellectual influence on the twentieth century, Freudian psychoanalysis. Sigmund Freud (1856–1939) provided the foundation for dream analysis. He posited that beneath the workings of the conscious mind there exists another layer of thought expression called the subconscious, or unconscious. When we dream, the conscious mind rests and the subconscious takes over. We have no control over what is revealed by the unconscious, but Freud believed that a person's true identity could be understood only by examining the interaction of both conscious and unconscious parts of the mind. For Freud also argued that the subconscious manifests itself continually: when we sleep, it takes over. But even when we are awake, the unconscious plays a major role in shaping how we feel, act, and think.

In 1900, Freud published *The Interpretation of Dreams*, a book that developed the theoretical framework for psychoanalysis, a method that would aid therapists in treating the emotional and psychological maladies of patients. Freud centered this analysis on the importance of understanding the interrelationship between a patient's childhood experiences, dreams, and current problems. When a literary critic applies these same principles to interpreting a work of literature, it is called psychoanalytic criticism. The literary critic is not interested in curing a patient's mental illness but in explaining why an author or one of his characters behaves in a certain way. According to this mode of analysis, a literary work must be interpreted just as a dream might be interpreted: as a complex puzzle that, when analyzed properly, reveals hidden motivations, symbolic patterns or designs, and a deeper appreciation of meanings and actions that were originally concealed.

Literary scholar Christopher Benfey, in tracing the extraordinary wealth of psychoanalytic readings of Poe, concluded that "no other writer other than Freud himself has so engaged the psychoanalytic literary community, from Marie Bonaparte's pioneering reading of Poe to Lacan's famous interpretation of 'The Purloined Letter' " (27). Marie Bonaparte conducted a Freudian inquiry into Poe's lifelong fixation on women as mother surrogates. She was perhaps first to argue that Poe's writings furnish overwhelming evidence of his sexual maladjustment, that he was impotent, and that his marriage to Virginia Clemm was never consummated. Marie Bonaparte's theories advanced earlier psychoanalytic readings such as Lorine Pruette's 1920 essay, "A Psychoanalytic Study of E.A. Poe," opened up a major vein of Poe criticism that would continue to interpret his works through various Freudian lenses. It should be obvious that anyone interested in studying the psychology of human aberration and neurosis would be drawn to the stories and poems of Edgar Allan Poe.

Poe's characters seldom reveal anything about their dream worlds, perhaps because so many of them demonstrate behavior where dream—or, more precisely, nightmare—has become reality, where subconscious urges and motivations have manifested themselves in conscious pursuits. The obsessive maladies inherent in Poe's characters have prompted several critics to suggest that Poe was particularly fascinated with schizophrenia, and that his protagonists possess traits associated with this mental illness in their collective inability to integrate the demands of personality with the demands of the external world, in their propensity for violence, and in their complete withdrawal from social and familial connections. It is even possible to argue that many of Poe's individual characters contain and dramatize all at once the contradictory impulses of the human psyche.

Most of Poe's canon is enriched through psychoanalytic interpretations of his themes and characterization, but how does psychoanalytic criticism help to illuminate the detective stories specifically? In the job of explaining and interpreting events that have occurred, Poe's detective would appear to function in a role that parallels that of the psychoanalyst. The psychoanalyst asks patients to talk about their problems, to recall situations, dreams, events, and emotions that were painful, confusing, and perhaps forgotten or repressed. In doing so, the patient helps the therapist to piece together a psychological portrait that can then be used to help explain neurotic behavior for which no physical cause can be discovered. Dupin is a criminologist, but he is also a master psychoanalyst. He, too, employs the piecing together of evidence, motivation, and inexplicable human behavior to create a pattern or model that explains criminal action. Both the psychoanalyst and the detective operate from rational orientations; they share a similar faith in the power of human reason to contain and solve serious problems.

Freud's most famous model of the human psyche—the tripartite design—divides the human mind into three parts: the id, the superego, and the ego. The irrational and destructive part Freud called the *id*. It contains our darkest urges, secret and repressed wishes, most intense fears and is connected to the libido—the repository of our psychosexual energies. The id is the most powerful component of the human psyche. Since it contains material that is both repressed and volatile, when the id does manifest itself either in dream or in conscious action, the effects are quite powerful. Freud initially believed that the human id, because it housed all of our infantile, hostile, and aggressive feelings, was a strictly negative part of the psyche. (This position eventually resulted in Carl Jung, Freud's most famous student, severing his relationship with his mentor; Jung believed that the unconscious also possessed positive energies that give birth to art, personal growth, and a shared bond with others.) To maintain control over the id's impulses, Freud postulated that another component of the psyche, the *superego*, acts as a kind of censor, designed primarily to protect both society and the individual from the ravages of the id. The superego is that element of the self that insulates social values and initiates moral judgments. It represents that part of the psyche that forces the individual to repress certain acts because they are wrong or destructive, thrusting them back into the subconscious. Essentially, the superego is the voice of our conscience, nagging us about behavior that is forbidden, often ending in guilt—the gift that goes on giving. The *ego*, on the other hand, is the rational and logical part of the waking mind. Freud argued that its job was to merge the instinctual urges of the id with the repressive demands of the superego, mediating a course of behavior that is both acceptable and nondestructive.

If a psychoanalytic critic were to apply Freud's tripartite model to Poe's detective fiction, Dupin emerges in possession of characteristics that resemble Freud's definition of the ego, that part of the psyche that regulates human behavior by asserting rational control over destructive and irrational impulses. If the criminal is linked to the id by way of his hostile and antisocial actions, then the police must be associated with the superego, or that element of the psyche that manifests itself through punishment and constraint. Dupin certainly possesses the imaginative attributes to explore the id by acknowledging the criminal's aggressive and violent proclivities, and he uses this knowledge to help him identify with the criminal mind (e.g., "The Purloined Letter"). Critic Peter Thomas even argues that Dupin has so much in common with the egotism of the criminals he pursues that the detective "emerges not as the criminal's polar opposite but as an ambiguous figure who shares that transgressor's desire for control" (70). On the other hand, Dupin also reinforces the status of the police, as the prefect supplies evidence to the detective and solicits his help in solving cases. While neither a policeman nor a murderer, Dupin operates in "harmony" with both—in fact taking on certain unique flavors of both—just as Freud believed the ego was situated to serve as a moderating force between the id and the superego. Like the ego in Freud's model, then, Dupin regulates the transgressive nature of the (criminal) id with the need for self-discipline and the maintenance of the social status quo associated with the (police) superego.

Although his reputation rests securely in the area of psychology, Freud was also an excellent literary critic, applying and uncovering elements of psychoanalysis in specific literary texts. For example, Freud's conceptualization of the Oedipal complex—the sexual attraction a male child maintains for his mother—originated from his reading of Sophocles' play, *Oedipus Rex*. Furthermore, Freud's understanding of the relationship between psychosomatic illness and repressed guilt was immeasurably influenced by Dostoevski's *The Brothers*

Karamazov. Freud subsequently wrote major essays on both Sophocles and Dostoevski, but oddly, the father of psychoanalysis never took up the subject of Edgar Allan Poe in his published writings. This exercise would be undertaken after Freud's death by one of his disciples, Jacques Lacan (1901–81), who was particularly fascinated with Poe's "The Purloined Letter." On April 26, 1955, as part of a year-long seminar that addressed aspects of Freudian psychoanalysis, Lacan delivered an essay that examined this Poe tale as a parable for Lacan's conception of psychoanalysis.

Lacan begins by dismissing "The Purloined Letter" as a simple police mystery. Since the criminal details are known from the start and the criminal himself is already identified, the story's meaning is found in the revelation of symbolic design. Lacan viewed himself as an analyst, not a literary critic, so his interpretation of Poe was shaped by his efforts to set a psychoanalytic frame around the text of "The Purloined Letter." Central to Lacan's reading is the conceptualization of the stolen letter as a "signifier," or the obsessive center of the tale around which the characters and the action of the story revolve. Lacan views the letter as a parallel to the human unconscious insofar as all the characters who come into knowledge of its existence are duly influenced by it: "[F]or each the letter is his unconscious. It is his unconscious with all its consequences; that is to say, that at each moment of the symbolic circuit each becomes another human being" (47). Lacan came to view the stolen letter as a powerful (fetish) object that continually transforms whoever possesses it. For instance, as soon as the Minister D steals the object he changes his position from an active, visible agent (the thief) to a passive, invisible one, as his power depends upon the *threat* of exposing the letter's contents rather than in its actual disclosure. Accordingly, "[I]n playing the part of the one who hides, he is obliged to don the role of the Queen" (44). While he began the story in a position of control, the longer he holds the letter the more he becomes its slave, as the importance of the letter comes to exert a possessive influence over Minister D.

Lacan argues that in a similar fashion Dupin is pulled into the obsessive dynamic of this action, and he is likewise forced "to follow the path of the signifier" (44) in his efforts to retrieve it. In trading the letter for money and treating the case as an act of personal revenge against the minister, Lacan feels that Dupin undermines the significance of the letter, making his own efforts inglorious. Whoever holds the letter is likewise affected by it: "[T]he displacement of the signifier determines the subjects in their acts" (60).

Lacan's symbolic reading of the letter as a transformative object suggests the power of Freud's conception of the unconscious. All of the characters in the story can be said to "lose" their identities as a result of contact with the letter. Its influence is so dramatic that it literally shapes the behavior of the characters involved, as their egos are overwhelmed by the talismanic properties of what the letter signifies. Perhaps, Lacan speculates, this is why Poe was careful never to reveal the actual contents of the letter itself. Its significance becomes more enlarged when the reader is open to limitless speculation. Like the contents of the letter itself, Freud's conception of the unconscious was as a repository of potential danger, infinite in scope, that was always threatening to put the individual in jeopardy.

The closer and deeper the reader searches for ways to understand Poe, his life as well as his work, the more viable a psychoanalytic interpretation becomes. In the end, perhaps the most important Poe—at least in terms of the fascination he continues to hold for modern readers and critics—is Poe the psychologist. For he speaks to readers in voices from just beyond the edge of dream and madness. Taken together, his stories form a documentary that is a chronicle of the ego dying in public. His own life might have benefited tremendously from several sessions with an analyst, as it was a disaster on a scale that could rival the worst of his tragic protagonists. Poe was America's first celebrity martyr, the patron saint of a cult of psychological disintegration. It should surprise no one that for nearly a hundred years, his readers have tended to apply various psychoanalytic interpretations in an effort to unlock the complex mysteries of Poe's world and its close analogies to the workings of the human psyche. The "Alternate Reading" section in this chapter poses merely two approaches to analyzing his fiction from this theoretical design. There are finally as many dimensions to a psychoanalytic reading of Poe as there are Freudian disciples.

Selected Bibliography

Note: All page numbers in the text, unless otherwise noted, refer to *Edgar Allan Poe: Poetry, Tales, and Selected Essays*. Ed. Patrick F. Quinn. 1984. Reprint, New York: Library of America, 1996.

BOOKS BY EDGAR ALLAN POE

Tamerlane and Other Poems (1827).
Al Aaraaf, Tamerlane and Poems (1829).
Poems (1831).
Narrative of Arthur Gordon Pym (1838).
Tales of the Grotesque and Arabesque (1840).
Tales (1845).
The Raven and Other Poems (1845).
Eureka (1848).

EDITIONS AND COLLECTIONS OF WORKS BY EDGAR ALLAN POE

The Works of the Late Edgar Allan Poe. 4 vols. Ed. Rufus Wilmot Griswold. New York: Redfield, 1850–56. [No longer in print.]
The Works of Edgar Allan Poe. 10 vols. Eds. Edmund Clarence Stedman and George Edward Woodberry. Chicago: Stone and Kimball, 1894–96. [No longer in print.]

The Complete Works of Edgar Allan Poe. 17 vols. Ed. James A. Harrison. New York: Thomas Y. Crowell and Company, 1902.

The Complete Tales and Poems of Edgar Allan Poe. Ed. Hervey Allen. Modern Library. 1938. Reprint, New York: Random House, 1975.

Selected Writings of Edgar Allan Poe. Ed. Edward H. Davison. Riverside Edition. Boston: Houghton Mifflin, 1956.

The Portable Poe. Ed. Philip V. Stern. New York: Viking/Penguin, 1977.

Selections from the Critical Writings of Edgar Allan Poe. Ed. F.C. Prescott. New York: Gordian Press, 1981.

Essays and Reviews. Ed. G.R. Thompson. New York: Library of America, 1984.

Collected Writings of Edgar Allan Poe. 4 vols. Ed. Burton R. Pollin. Boston: Twayne, 1981 (vol. 1); New York: Gordian Press, 1985–86 (vols. 2, 3, 4).

The Complete Stories. New York: Everyman's Library/Alfred A. Knopf, 1992.

Closed on Account of Rabies: Poems and Tales of Edgar Allan Poe. Produced by Hal Willner. Mercury Records, 1997.

Thirty-Two Stories. Eds. Stuart Levine and Susan F. Levine. Indianapolis, Indiana: Hackett Publishing Company, 2000.

Tales of Mystery and Imagination. Secaucus, New Jersey: Castle, n.d.

LITERARY ANTHOLOGIES CONTAINING REPRESENTATIVE SELECTIONS OF WORK BY EDGAR ALLAN POE

American Gothic: An Anthology, 1787–1916. Ed. Charles L. Crow. Malden, Massachusetts, 1999.

Anthology of American Literature. Vol. 1. Ed. George McMichael. New York: Macmillan.

The Harper American Literature. Compact Volume. Ed. Donald McQuade. New York: HarperCollins.

Norton Anthology of American Literature. Vol. 1. Ed. Nina Baym. New York: W.W. Norton and Company.

SELECTED BIOGRAPHIES AND BIOCRITICAL STUDIES ON EDGAR ALLAN POE

Baudelaire, Charles. *The Painter of Modern Life.* Trans. Jonathan Mayne. New York: Phaidon Press/Da Capo Press, 1964.

Bittner, William. *Poe: A Biography.* Boston: Little, Brown and Company, 1962. [Out of print.]

Bonaparte, Marie. *The Life and Works of Edgar Poe: A Psychoanalytic Interpretation.* Trans. John Rodker. London: Hogarth Press, 1949.

Krutch, Joseph Wood. *Edgar Allan Poe: A Study in Genius.* New York: Alfred A. Knopf, 1926. [Out of print.]

Quinn, Arthur Hobson. *Edgar Allan Poe*. New York: Cooper Square Publishers, 1969.

Silverman, Kenneth. *Edgar A. Poe: Mournful and Never-Ending Remembrance*. New York: HarperCollins, 1991.

Symons, Julian. *The Tell-Tale Heart: The Life and Works of Edgar Allan Poe*. New York: Harper and Row, 1978.

Thomas, Dwight, and David J. Jackson. *The Poe Log: A Documentary Life of Edgar Allan Poe, 1809–1849*. Boston: G.K. Hall and Company, 1987.

Walter, Georges. *Edgar Poe*. Paris: Flammarion, 1991.

SELECTED POE BIBLIOGRAPHIES AND OTHER REFERENCE SOURCES

Carlson, Eric W. *A Companion to Poe Studies*. Westport, Connecticut: Greenwood Press, 1996.

Dameron, J. Lasley, and Louis Charles Stagg. *An Index to Poe's Critical Vocabulary*. Hartford, Connecticut: Transcendental Books, 1966.

Frank, Frederick S., and Anthony Magistrale. *The Poe Encyclopedia*. Westport, Connecticut: Greenwood Press, 1997.

Gale, Robert. *Plots and Characters in the Fiction and Poetry of Edgar Allan Poe*. Hamden, Connecticut: Archon, 1970.

Haining, Peter, ed. *The Edgar Allan Poe Scrapbook: Articles, Essays, Letters, Anecdotes, Photographs, and Memorabilia about the Legendary American Genius*. New York: Schocken Books, 1978.

Hammond, J.R. *An Edgar Allan Poe Companion*. New York: Barnes and Noble, 1981.

Hyneman, Esther F. *Edgar Allan Poe: An Annotated Bibliography of Books and Articles in English, 1827–1973*. Boston: G.K. Hall, 1974.

Ostrom, John Ward, ed. *The Letters of Edgar Allan Poe*. New York: Gordian Press, 1966.

Pollin, Burton R. *Word Index to Poe's Fiction*. New York: Gordian Press, 1982.

———. *Images of Poe's Works: A Comprehensive Descriptive Catalogue of Illustrations*. Westport, Connecticut: Greenwood Press, 1989.

Robbins, J. Albert. *Checklist of Edgar Allan Poe*. Columbus, Ohio: Charles E. Merrill, 1969.

Smith, Don G. *The Poe Cinema: A Critical Filmography of Theatrical Releases Based on the Works of Edgar Allan Poe*. Jefferson, North Carolina: McFarland, 1999.

Wiley, Elizabeth. *Concordance to the Poetry of Edgar Allan Poe*. Selinsgrove, Pennsylvania: Susquehanna University Press, 1989.

SELECTED CRITICISM I

CONTEMPORARY REVIEWS OF POE'S LIFE AND WORK

"The American Library." *Blackwood's Magazine*, November 1847, 574–92.

"American Poetry." *Frazer's Magazine*, July 1850, 17–19.

"Autographs." *New York Mirror*, January 1, 1842, 3.

Colton, George. "Poe's Tales." *The American Review*, September 1845, 306–9.

"Criticism of Poe's *Raven*." *New York Mirror*, April 26, 1845, 42–43.

"Death of Edgar A. Poe." *Baltimore Evening Sun*, October 8, 1849, 2.

"Death of Edgar Allan Poe." *Literary World*, October 13, 1849, 319.

"Death of Edgar Allan Poe." *New York Journal of Commerce*, October 9, 1849, 2.

Duyckinck, Evert. "Bryant's American Poets." *Arcturus*, 1840, 24–29.

———. "The Literary Prospects of 1845." *American Review*, February 1845, 146–51.

"E.A. Poe's New Work." *The Southern Literary Messenger*, January 1840, 126.

Fuller, Margaret. "Tales by Edgar A. Poe." *New York Daily Tribune*, July 11, 1845.

Griswold, Rufus Wilmot. "The Chief Tale Writers of America." *Washington National Intelligencer*, August 30, 1845.

———. [signed Lugwig] "The Death of Edgar A. Poe." *New York Daily Tribune*, October 9, 1849.

———. "Edgar A. Poe." *Poets and Poetry of America*. Philadelphia: Carey and Hart, 1842, 387.

Hewitt, John Hill. "A Poe Mystery Uncovered: The Lost 'Minerva' Review of 'Al Aaraaf'." *Minerva*, 1830 (?).

Lowell, James Russell. "Edgar A. Poe." *Graham's Magazine*, February 1845, 49–52.

———. "Introduction." *Pioneer*, January 1843, 1–3.

"Necessity for a National Literature." *Knickerbocker*, May 1845, 415–23.

"Notes to Men of Note." *New York Mirror*, July 5, 1845, 201.

[Review of] "*Pym's Adventures and Discoveries*." *New York Mirror*, August 11, 1838, 55.

[Review of] "*The Raven and Other Poems*." *Athenaeum*, February 28, 1846, 215–16.

[Review of] "*Tales*. By Edgar A. Poe." *Littell's Living Age*, November 15, 1845, 343.

[Review of] "*Tales*. By Edgar A. Poe." *Graham's Magazine*, September 1845, 143.

Tasistro, Louis Fitzgerald. "A Notice of Poe's Tales." *New York Daily Mirror*, December 28, 1839, 215.

BOOKS ABOUT EDGAR ALLAN POE

Bloom, Clive. *Reading Poe/Reading Freud: The Romantic Imagination in Crisis*. New York: St. Martin's Press, 1988.

Carlson, Eric W., ed. *Critical Essays on Edgar Allan Poe*. Boston: G.K. Hall and Company, 1987.

Dayan, Joan. *Fables of the Mind: An Inquiry in Poe's Fiction*. Oxford: Oxford University Press, 1987.

Grossman, Joan Delaney. *Edgar Allan Poe in Russia: A Study in Legend and Literary Influence*. Würzburg, Germany: Jal-Verlag, 1973.

Hansen, Thomas, with Burton R. Pollin. *The German Face of Edgar Allan Poe: A Study of Literary References in His Works*. Columbia, South Carolina: Camden House, 1995.

Hoffman, Daniel. *Poe Poe Poe Poe Poe Poe Poe*. Garden City, New York: Doubleday, 1972.

Hyslop, Lois, and Francis E., eds. *Baudelaire on Poe*. State College, Pennsylvania: Pennsylvania State University Press, 1952.

Kesterson, David B., ed. *Critics on Poe*. Coral Gables, Florida: Miami University Press, 1973.

Knapp, Bettina L. *Edgar Allan Poe*. New York: Frederick Unger Publishing, 1984.

Magistrale, Tony, and Sidney Poger. *Poe's Children: Connections Between Tales of Terror and Detection*. New York: Peter Lang Publishing, 1999.

May, Charles. *Edgar Allan Poe: A Study of the Short Fiction*. Boston: Twayne, 1991.

Muller, John P., and William J. Richardson, eds. *The Purloined Poe: Lacan, Derrida, and Psychoanalytic Reading*. Baltimore, Maryland: Johns Hopkins University Press, 1988.

Phillips, Elizabeth. *Edgar Allan Poe: An American Imagination*. Port Washington, New York: Kennikat Press, 1979.

Regan, Robert, ed. *Poe: A Collection of Critical Essays*. Englewood Cliffs, New Jersey: Prentice-Hall, 1967.

Rosenheim, Shawn, and Stephen Rachman, eds. *The American Face of Edgar Allan Poe*. Baltimore, Maryland: Johns Hopkins University Press, 1995.

Silverman, Kenneth, ed. *New Essays on Poe's Major Tales*. 1993. Reprint, New York: Cambridge University Press, 1998.

Vines, Lois Davis, ed. *Poe Abroad: Influence, Reputation, Affinities*. Iowa City, Iowa: University of Iowa Press, 1999.

Walsh, John E. *Poe the Detective*. New Brunswick, New Jersey: Rutgers University Press, 1968.

Williams, Michael J.S. *A World of Words: Language and Displacement in the Fiction of Edgar Allan Poe*. Durham, North Carolina: Duke University Press, 1988.

ARTICLES AND PARTS OF BOOKS ABOUT EDGAR ALLAN POE

Andriano, Joseph. "Archetypal Projection in 'Ligeia': A Post-Jungian Reading." *Poe Studies* 19 (1986): 176–85.

Barker, Clive, and Stephen Jones. *Clive Barker's A–Z of Horror*. New York: Harper Prism, 1997.

Benfey, Christopher. "Poe and the Unreadable: 'The Black Cat' and 'The Tell-Tale Heart'." *New Essays on Poe's Major Tales*. Ed. Kenneth Silverman. New York: Cambridge University Press, 1993. Pp. 27–44.

Bieganowski, Ronald. "The Self-Consuming Narrator in Poe's 'Ligeia' and 'Usher.' " *American Literature* 60 (1988): 175–87.

Bloom, Harold. *Poetics of Influence*. New Haven: Schwab, 1988.

Boyle, Eloise M. "Poe in Russia." *Poe Abroad: Influences, Reputation, Affinities*. Ed. Lois Davis Vines. Iowa City, Iowa: University of Iowa Press, 1999. Pp. 19–30.

Brand, Dana. " 'Reconstructing the Flâneur': Poe's Invention of the Detective Story." *Genre* 18 (1985): 35–56.

Brophy, Brigid. "Detective Fiction: A Modern Myth of Violence." *Hudson Review* 18 (1965): 11–30.

Creed, Barbara. "Horror and the Carnivalesque." *Fields of Vision: Essays in Film Studies.* Eds. Leslie Devereaux and Roger Hillman. Berkeley, California: University of California Press, 1995. Pp. 127–59.

Edmundson, Mark. *Nightmare on Main Street: Angels, Sadomasochism, and the Culture of the Gothic.* Cambridge, Massachusetts: Harvard University Press, 1997.

Fiedler, Leslie A. *Waiting for the End.* New York: Dell, 1964.

Forclaz, Roger. "Psychoanalysis and Edgar Allan Poe: A Critique of the Bonaparte Thesis." *Critical Essays on Edgar Allan Poe.* Ed. Eric W. Carlson. Boston: G.K. Hall and Company, 1987. Pp. 187–95.

Frank, Frederick S. "The Gothic Romance, 1762–1824." *Horror Literature: An Historical Survey and Critical Guide to the Best of Horror.* Ed. Marshall Tymn. New York: R.R. Bowker Company, 1981. Pp. 3–34.

Fukuchi, Curtis. "Repression and Guilt in Poe's 'Morella.' " *Studies in Short Fiction* 24 (1987): 149–54.

Gargano, James. "The Question of Poe's Narrators." *College English* 25 (1963): 177–81.

Garrison, Joseph M., Jr. "The Function of Terror in the Work of Edgar Allan Poe." *American Quarterly* 18 (1960): 136–50.

Hampson, Norman. *The Enlightenment: An Evaluation of Its Assumptions, Attitudes, and Values.* London: Penguin, 1968.

Hirsch, David H. "The Pit and the Apocalypse." *Sewanee Review* 76 (1968): 632–52.

Hoffman, Frederick J. *The 20's: American Writing in the Postwar Decade.* New York: Macmillan, 1949.

Jullian, Philippe. *The Symbolists.* New York: E.P. Dutton, 1975.

Kennedy, J. Gerald. "Poe, 'Ligeia,' and the Problem of Dying Women." *New Essays on Poe's Major Tales.* Ed. Kenneth Silverman. New York: Cambridge University Press, 1993. Pp. 113–30.

Lacan, Jacques. "Seminar on 'The Purloined Letter.' " Trans. Jeffrey Mehlman. *The Purloined Poe: Lacan, Derrida, and Psychoanalytic Reading.* Eds. John P. Muller and William J. Richardson. 1988. Reprint, Baltimore, Maryland: Johns Hopkins University Press, 1993. Pp. 28–54.

Lawler, James. "Daemons of the Intellect: The Symbolists and Poe." *Critical Inquiry* 14 (Autumn 1987): 95–110.

Lawrence, D.H. "Edgar Allan Poe." *Studies in Classic American Literature.* 1923. Reprint, New York: Penguin, 1981. Pp. 70–88.

Lemay, J.L. Leo. "The Psychology of 'The Murders in the Rue Morgue.' " *American Literature* 54 (1983): 165–88.

Lippit, Noriko Mizuta. "Poe in Japan." *Poe Abroad: Influences, Reputation, Affinities.* Ed. Lois Davis Vines. Iowa City, Iowa: University of Iowa Press, 1999.

Lovecraft, Howard Phillips. *Supernatural Horror in Literature.* New York: Ben Abramson. 1945. Reprint, New York: Dover Publications, 1973.

Mallin, Dea Adria. "Edgar Allan Poe: Descent in Madness." *Creativity and Madness: Psychological Studies of Art and Artists*. Ed. Barry M Painter, et al. Burbank, California: Aimed Press, 1995. Pp. 111–34,

Oates, Joyce Carol. "Afterword: Reflections on the Grotesque." *Haunted: Tales of the Grotesque*. New York: Dutton, 1994. Pp. 303–7.

Panek, Leroy Lad. *An Introduction to the Detective Story*. Bowling Green, Ohio: Bowling Green State University Popular Press, 1987.

Pollin, Burton R. "Poe's 'Murders in the Rue Morgue': The Ingenious Web Unravelled." *Studies in the American Renaissance*. Ed. Joel Meyerson. Boston: G.K. Hall and Company, 1977. Pp. 235–59.

Pruette, Lorine. "A Psychoanalytic Study of E.A. Poe." *American Journal of Psychology* 31 (1920): 370–402.

Reeder, Roberta. " 'The Black Cat' as a Study in Repression." *Poe Studies* 7 (1974): 20–21.

Tate, Allen. "Our Cousin, Mr. Poe." *Poe: A Collection of Critical Essays*. Ed. Robert Regan. Englewood Cliffs, New Jersey: Prentice-Hall, 1967. Pp. 38–50.

Thoms, Peter. *Detection and Its Designs: Narrative and Power in 19th-Century Detective Fiction*. Athens, Ohio: Ohio University Press, 1998.

Twitchell, James B. *The Living Dead: A Study of the Vampire in Romantic Literature*. Durham, North Carolina: Duke University Press, 1981.

Underwood, Tim, and Chuck Miller, eds. *Bare Bones: Conversations on Terror with Stephen King*. New York: McGraw-Hill, 1988.

Vidal, Gore. *Palimpsest: A Memoir*. New York: Random House, 1995.

Vines, Lois Davis. "Charles Baudelaire." *Poe Abroad: Influences, Reputation, Affinities*. Ed. Lois Davis Vines. Iowa City, Iowa: University of Iowa Press, 1999. Pp. 165–70.

Zanger, Jules. "Poe's 'Berenice': Philosophical Fantasy and Its Pitfalls." *The Scope of the Fantastic—Theory, Technique, Major Authors*. Ed. Robert A. Collins and Howard D. Pearce. Westport, Connecticut: Greenwood Press, 1985. Pp. 135–42.

Index

About the Author

TONY MAGISTRALE is Professor of English and Director of Undergraduate
Advising at the University of Vermont. He has published extensively in the
field of Gothic Studies including two books on Poe, *The Poe Encyclopedia*
(Greenwood 1997) and *Poe's Children: Connections Between Tales of Terror and
Detection* (1999). He is also the author of *The Dark Descent: Essays Defining
Stephen King's Horrorscape* (Greenwood 1992).